Make Every Day a
FRIDAY!

Kudos for Make Every Day a Friday!

"*Make Every Day a Friday!* is as clear and concise as it is accessible and supportive. With step-by-step guidance, it provides valuable spiritual lessons during times of growth and change."

—Marci Shimoff, NY Times bestselling author of *Happy for No Reason, Chicken Soup for the Women's Soul* and featured teacher in The Secret.

"*Make Everyday a Friday!* is both inspiring and practical. I recommend this book as a companion for any woman walking through major changes in her life."

—Shakti Gawain, author *Creative Visualization* and *Living In The Light*

"If you're even thinking of changing careers, you've got to read this book. *Make Every Day a Friday!* could also be called Make Career Change Fun. This deeply inspiring book is filled with savvy advice, powerful tools, and amazing support. Marina writes as if she's coaching you personally. I highly recommend it to every job career changer, including men."

—Barbara Stanny, author of *Secrets of Six-Figure Women* and *Overcoming Underearning*

"If you are thinking about a career change, read this book first."

—Cindy Cashman million selling author
CindyCashman.com

"Women will find the material and thought provoking questions revealing and helpful."

—Fran Hewitt, co-author of *The Power of Focus for Women: How to Live the Life You Really Want*

"Marina Spence's, *Make Every Day a Friday!* is a down-to-earth guide for any woman (or man) who wants to pursue their passion to do something different. The challenges appear to be daunting but Marina has a plan that should help those who don't know or who aren't sure about how to start. This is a must read for those contemplating a major change."

—Phyllis May, author of *ReFIRED Not Retired...Re-ignite Your Zest for Life*

"Make Every Day A Friday! is a quick read that gets to the heart of making big changes in our lives. As a consultant and an author, Marina has created a laser-focused process to get straight to the areas where you might be stopped and steps you through what you need to do to create the life you've dreamt of. It is a must read for all women (and men!) who are searching for meaning through work and having the life that suits us best!"

—Dr. Natalie L. Petouhoff, author of *Smart Inventors Finish Rich: Ten Steps to Reaching the American Dream*

"Marina weaves into her practical and though-provoking book many useful tools for women in mid-life who are contemplating a career change. It is full of wisdom and real experiences of women who have gone through the process using Marina's step-by-step guidance."

—Tuyet Cong-Ton-Nu, Certified Nutrition
Consultant, www.NourishingPath.com

"Marina is your guide through the often murky mental world of job changing. She walks you through each step with a friendly, encouraging tone. You are not alone in your journey to find what satisfies you. I wish I'd had this resource and wisdom when I was trying to figure out what work suited me better."

—Jennifer Flaa, CEO, Vettanna LLC
(www.vettanna.com) and Vocalist, Urban
Fiction (www.urbanfictionmusic.com)

"Marina Spence's *Make Every Day a Friday!* validates the long, circuitous process I have been through in the past few years as I searched for a meaningful career. It would have been great if I could have read it at the beginning of the process!"

—Linda Jay Geldens, Copyeditor/Copywriter,
www.LindaJayGeldens.com

Make Every Day a
FRIDAY!

The joy of connecting who you are
with what you do

Marina Spence

NEW YORK

Make Every Day a

FRIDAY!

By Marina Spence

ISBN: 978-1-60037-450-0 Paperback

Published by:

MORGAN · JAMES
THE ENTREPRENEURIAL PUBLISHER™

Morgan James Publishing, LLC
1225 Franklin Ave Ste 325
Garden City, NY 11530-1693
Toll Free 800-485-4943
www.MorganJamesPublishing.com

Front Cover Design by:
Sam Tomasello
www.SciencePiction.com

**Cover Wrap Layout &
Interior Design by:**
Heather Kirk
www.GraphicsByHeather.com
Heather@GraphicsByHeather.com

Habitat
for Humanity®
Peninsula
Building Partner

This book is dedicated to every woman who struggles with expressing herself through career

and

to my mother, Inez Spence, my first role model in career change, and so much more.

A portion of the proceeds of this book goes to Women for Women International, an acclaimed non-profit that assists women victims of war. Please consider changing a woman's life by sponsoring her.

Visit www.WomenForWomen.org.

Contents

PART 3: MOVING ON 103

Introduction

How can you design your life so that you never, ever again experience that horrid, dreaded realization that it's Monday already? So that you never have to wrench yourself out of bed to get ready for work? So that you never feel the knot that comes in your stomach when you think of another week at your job?

My answer: find work that you enjoy and that fulfills you. Maybe it's a new job or a new career. It could even be the job you have now, but with a new you doing it; a person who knows her passions, her purpose, and who has a plan.

This is a book about career changes. It is written for the woman who wants to discover the best way to express herself through her work. I describe a system of career change that starts from the inside out, meaning connecting *who you are to what you do.*

Why does this connection matter? When we find a match between who we are inwardly and what we do outwardly, we become happier, more powerful, and can make a real contribution to the world.   And Mondays are no longer Mondays; every day is a Friday.

Who doesn't want all of that?

Change can be mysterious, exciting, and full of possibility, so in this book you'll read about the joy of change. And since change causes many of us to feel apprehensive, uncertain, and anxious, you'll also learn ways to manage the stress of change. They are all simple.

My own careers have brought me adventures and joys that I could not have imagined as a girl—a girl who thought she could only choose between being a teacher or a nurse. While these are two worthy professions, happily we live in times with more options. I have found fulfillment through finding a "right" career and then changing, twice, to new careers. I want to empower other women to do the same: to imagine. To discover. To change, if that's what you want to do.

I also write about career change because we spend so much time at work. Since where we spend our time is where we spend our precious energy, career has the potential of being an energy drain or an energy giver. When we become energized by our career, we energize our world. We all win!

How Much Time Do You Spend Working?

Let's dive right into a simple exercise. Do you know how many hours a week you spend on work and work-related activities? (If you do, feel free to skip this exercise.) You prepare for work, commute to and from, work, and then unwind. Many women also bring work home or wake up at night worrying about work. If you are a full-time mom, you definitely bring your work home with you!

Please write down below how many hours you spend *per day* and then *per week* on work and work-related activities. Be sure to include preparation, the commute, and worry time. If your work schedule is irregular, just use an average.

For example, I used to spend one hour per day preparing for work, two hours commuting, ten hours at work, and roughly one hour unwinding. (For the job I'm using in this example, I did not bring work home and rarely thought about work once it was over.) That gave me a total of fourteen hours per day. 14 hours per day x 5 work days per week = 70 hours per week on work-related activities.

_____ Your daily estimate (preparation + commute + work + unwind + work at home + worry)

_____ Number of days per week

_____ Your weekly estimate

Now, please write down how many hours you spend per week sleeping—you know, that necessary activity that heals and refreshes. To estimate, average your nightly hours and multiply by seven. Be sure to average, since you may sleep longer on weekends than during the week.

_____ Your weekly estimate of sleep hours

Now add your work-related hours to sleep hours and subtract it from the total hours in a week, 168 (24 x 7).

When I first did this, I got forty-eight. Wow! I only had forty-eight hours a week for friends, family, spiritual practice, walking the dog, email, movies, volunteer work, reading, eating, exercise, cleaning, special projects, paying bills, shopping, etc. More time was spent on work than anything else!

If work is (or soon will be) your top time-grabber, why not make it as enjoyable and meaningful as possible? Why not choose to do something that you—as incredible as it might seem—would do even if you weren't paid for it? (But you still had a means of support, of course.)

After reading this book, you might find yourself changing careers. Or maybe a career tweak is enough. Whatever you do or don't do, I'll guide you to make your changes from the power of your inner, deeper self.

The Career Change Epidemic

Career dissatisfaction seems to be an epidemic. How many women do you know who are happy—vibrantly, enthusiastically happy —with their careers? Think of your five closest friends. How many of them are looking for new jobs? How many do you think will be in the same job this time next year? How many are dreaming of a new career?

A 2007 Reuters survey says that sixty percent of workers in the United States have either recently made a career change or are planning one. That makes changing careers more popular than marriage![1] If you are considering making a career move, take heart in the fact that YOU ARE NOT ALONE.

Why Women?

Are more women dissatisfied now with their career than ever before? I don't know. Careers and the freedom to choose careers is still relatively new for women; if your grandmother had a vibrant career she was probably ahead of her time, and unusual.

National Public Radio has a segment called "This I Believe" during which listeners write or call in their strongly held beliefs. Since this is my book, this is my "This I Believe" segment.

I believe that if more women felt *fulfilled* in their careers, the world would be a better place.

---

1 According to 2006 U.S. Census Bureau data, less than fifty percent of American households are in traditional, male-female marriages.

What do I mean by fulfilled?

I don't mean achieving higher status, earning more money, or gaining more power. I'm certainly not against those achievements; I'd like more myself! But I'm old enough to know that they don't bring deep-down satisfaction, nor do they necessarily improve the world as a whole.

The Oxford Dictionary says that fulfilling one's self means developing one's gifts to the full. In a fulfilling career your needs are met and your gifts are shared with others. Fulfilled means that who you are connects with what you do, and that the inner you has found its place in the outer world.

I believe that women can lead the way in creating fulfilling work, and by doing this, can lead the way to creating a better planet.

Am I being too simplistic to think that a...

> Woman more fulfilled with career →
> Greater happiness → Positively affecting
> those she influences → Circle of fulfillment
> and happiness expands

Recall what it's like to be around someone who's genuinely positive and upbeat when you aren't feeling that way. Did you go away feeling uplifted? Yes, and that's what I'm talking about. It's an epidemic of good health. Instead of spreading a virus, we can spread the experience of joy, purpose, and fulfillment.

But why women? Why should women be the leaders in creating fulfilling work that leads to a better world for all of us?

First, we are less tied to the traditional ways of working than men, so we are more likely to try something truly new. We haven't been the ones leading the corporations. We haven't led the government. We haven't led the universities. We certainly haven't led the army. We are less invested in keeping things the way they are.

Second, just as we haven't led in traditional workplaces, we have benefited from them less. And people who have less to lose usually are freer to create change.

In the United States, after years of equal employment laws and lawsuits, a woman now earns just seventy-seven cents for every dollar that her male counterpart earns.[2] But it's not just money that motivates us. A 2006 survey shows that women are leaving corporate jobs for entrepreneurship at two times the rate of men.[3] Why? Some say it's because corporate life is not amenable to balancing work and home. But the top reason executive-level women left was to take risks and to test their personal limits.[4] In other words, women leave to grow.

Finally, women can lead the way to fulfilling work because we tend to be more aware of our feelings and more likely to value them than men. It's this "feeling" dimension that adds meaning to many of our lives, and it's generally been missing from the workplace. Whose idea was it that "feelings" have no place in a productive work situation? Well, most likely it wasn't a woman's.

As girls, we were socialized to talk about our feelings and about relationships. Having this permission means we are often quicker on the uptake than a man is to know that a particular job is untenable for us—that we don't *feel* good about it. And we are also quicker to know when something at the workplace needs to change. If we are bold and willing to

---

2 Institute for Women's Policy Research, 2005
3 Cheskin Research, 2006
4 Survey by Korn/Ferry International, Columbia Business School, and Duran Group, 2001

stand up against the status quo, we can try to change how our workplace works. If that's not right, we can change our workplace altogether.

Many women are more willing to admit that something in the world these days just doesn't "feel right." We don't need much more than that to support a change. We don't need the studies or the statistics. We are willing to do something new because it "feels like the right thing to do."

How This Book Can Lead to Fulfilling Work

This book is a "how-to" guide that reveals:

+ Career myths that make you feel crazy if you believe them

+ How to know whether your angst comes from being in the wrong career, or something else

+ How to begin or further your discovery of your heart's purpose: who you are

+ How to assess your current career in light of your heart's purpose

+ How to change careers, if that's what you decide, in the way that is right for you—gradually and gracefully or with emergency precision

+ How to use the inner secrets of change to guide your career changes

The book provides many exercises to help you achieve these goals. You can complete the exercises as you go, or you might want to read the book straight through and return to the exercises after finishing. It's up to you.

Who Are You?

I wrote this book for anyone who works and who cares about making the most of her career. You might be a:

+ College student facing her first career
+ Mom who works for her family and is re-entering the outside work force
+ Baby Boomer burnt to a crisp with a job she has outgrown
+ Senior wanting to pass on her wisdom and
+ Anywhere in between

Anyone can read this book and benefit from it. But if you are a guy, here's one warning: I had to learn what seemed like hundreds of sports and war metaphors in order to function in the corporate world (some of which I like, such as "my bad"). The metaphors you'll read in this book are my revenge.

Stress–Free Career Change Phases

Following this introduction, **Part 1: Discovery** describes some of my early career lessons, explores career myths, and guides you through assessing your work situation. Are you connecting *who you are* to *what you do*? If not, what and where is the discrepancy and what do you want to do about it?

When facing change, it almost always helps to return to the beginning: to the simplest of needs and joys, to where we started and what we hoped for right from the start. I begin Part 1 of this book with stories from my first job, babysitting. I do this because, while babysitting, I learned seven lessons of career change that have never been proven outdated. When you read about my first job, I hope that you remember your own early work and what you learned from it.

Someone told me the story of her friend who was in the midst of career despondency. She hated her job but didn't know what else to do. Another friend asked one simple question, "When you were little, what did you want to be when you grew up?" The woman remembered that she had always wanted to be a doctor, a specific type of doctor. Two years later she enrolled in Harvard Medical School. She now works in Alaska fulfilling her childhood dream of working with Native Alaskans.

Being a doctor might not be your dream. Whatever it is, Part 1 will help you remember.

Part 2: Zooming In helps you answer questions like, "What do you want to do for a living? What are the steps you need to take to realize your goal? How long will your new career journey take? How can you best plan and prepare?"

In **Part 3: Moving On**, you'll see how to move on to a new career or a new phase of your current career with style.

In each part of the book, you'll receive an inner key to change. If you use these keys, they will open the doors to what you need and what is needed from you. The keys are:

+ **Tuning in**—"Tuning in" is a simple way to quiet your mind, so that deeper understanding can emerge. It also develops focus and detachment.

+ **Noticing**—Through "Noticing" you can watch your thoughts without judgment—and even watch them disappear. By "noticing" your thoughts without the distractions of emotion and judgment, you will be freer to recognize what is truly important.

+ **Just knowing**—The first two inner keys bring us to the final and most important. "Just knowing" is how we recognize our own voice as it speaks to us from behind all the distractions of our mind and the world. With this key, you have an unbeatable inner compass: your own intuition. It points the way to your destination, giving you shortcuts and time-savers along the way.

Your Guides

In this book you'll not only hear my story of how I connected who I am with what I do, but you'll meet five women whom I've mentored. While their real names have been changed to ensure privacy, their experiences have not.

Let's meet two of them now through "before" pictures.

Allison told me, with the sincerity of the wounded, "Marina, I hate my job. I hate my career. I have got to get out!"

She said she woke up on weekday mornings covered with a blanket of dread. Getting out of bed at the last possible minute, she pushed herself out the door with two cups of coffee. Once at work, she rewarded herself with a bagel, and then edged through the day with her eyes on the weekend.

* * *

Unlike Allison, Rachel liked her job. And, why not? Her career had been good to her. Diligently working her way up, she now felt comfortable and secure. But Rachel also had a nagging feeling that she could do more with her life. She had no idea what.

While hearing other people's stories is instructive, the real guide of this book is your intuition. As you read, listen to it. It's the inner feeling that senses what will uplift your spirit and feed your soul, and directs you toward that. Your intuition isn't your thoughts, particularly your same-old, same-old thoughts. It's softer and quieter, and is always waiting for you to listen.

If You Want More

You will also find that almost every chapter could be a book by itself— but who has time to read that much? So I chose a broader approach, knowing that we can always dig deeper in one of two ways.

1. First, I welcome you to my company's website, www.PinkEdge.com, for more resources than would fit in *Make Every Day a Friday!* Simply select "free stuff" from The Pink Edge home page.

2. Join a Pink Edge telecourse to design and try on your new career in the stress-free way. I've made the telecourse easy for you to take; please see the Special Offer at the end of this book.

Most of all, I congratulate you for being open to exploring change, and look forward to meeting or hearing from you soon.

To your fabulous career success!

Marina

marina@pinkedge.com

PART 1
Discovery

1:
Seven Lessons from Babysitting

I grew up in a Northern California town where locking doors at night, at least in the early 1960s, was optional. The neighborhood was a small town within a small town; you might not like your neighbors, but you did know them.

When Mrs. King, our next-door neighbor, first needed a babysitter, she asked my mother if my older sister could help out. Since the babysitting job was on a school night, my mother said no; my sister, who had just been diagnosed with poor vision in one eye, needed extra time for homework. But I was available and, by default, became a babysitter. I was not quite twelve.

I remember feeling nervous just before my first night. What if the two kids didn't listen to me? What if they were still awake when the Kings came home? What if…what if…what if…?

> Babysitting Lesson #1: It's normal to be scared when starting a new career.

My worries evaporated the first night; babysitting was a dream job. I babysat for the best-behaved kids in the state of

California. Roger, age seven, and his four-year-old sister, Carol, did what I said, when I said it. After playing with them and reading them to sleep at their 8 P.M. bedtime, I read my own book and rummaged through the cupboards for what food I could take without Mrs. King noticing it was gone. At ten o'clock, I watched "The Carol Burnett Show" and counted up how much money I would earn.

For this "work," I earned thirty-five cents per hour. That meant I had money to buy vanilla cokes and MAD magazines without having to ask my parents! Beyond the thrill of independence, I knew my parents worried about the envelopes in the "To Pay" section of the file organizer; their fears clung to me like paper clips to a magnet. Less allowance for me meant more for *the bills*.

Who could be luckier? I had fun and helped out my parents at the same time.

> Babysitting Lesson #2: Work can be fun!

> Babysitting Lesson #3: Having money is great!

An Angry Boss

One summer day after a babysitting evening, Mrs. King came over. As my mother opened the front screen door, I heard Mrs. King say, in her distinctive South Carolina drawl, "I'm going to wring your daughter's neck."

Thinking she was talking about my younger sister, who had a talent for trouble, I was about to step into the kitchen from the living room to say hello. But her next words stopped me.

"She should have told me that my father called last night! I didn't know it until just now, when he called back."

Then I remembered the telephone call that I had received last night. It went something like this:

ME: Hello?

HIM: Is Lydia there?

ME: Umm, no...(I wondered, should I say I was the babysitter? Mrs. King never told me what to do when the telephone rang. Should I take a message? I looked around for a message pad but didn't see one.)

HIM: Never mind. I'll call back later.

Click.

I went back to watching television and keeping myself awake, since my new worst fear was having the Kings come home at 11 P.M. and finding me asleep on their couch. I forgot to tell them about the call.

During Mrs. King's angry visit, I hid in our living room, expecting my mom to stand up for me. Instead, she calmed Mrs. King down by listening and sympathizing. Later, she asked me if I had been listening to Mrs. King and, when I said yes, that was that.

But I wasn't satisfied. "What's the big deal?" I grumbled to myself. "Her dad called her back. She should have shown me how to answer the phone!"

> Babysitting Lesson #4: Bosses can sometimes be unfair.

Mrs. King quickly forgot about being angry. The next week she showed me how to answer the phone and take messages.

After a few more months of babysitting, I discovered that other babysitters in the neighborhood received fifty cents per hour, not thirty-five. I told my mom. She must have mentioned it to Mrs. King, for she raised my pay to match.

> Babysitting Lesson #5: Get paid what you are worth.

Comfort Zones

After the Kings moved back to South Carolina, I babysat for other neighborhood moms. During the summers, my sisters and I also worked in our home following a checklist that mother left every day before work.

But working in other people's homes was an eye-opener. Each house in the subdivision was designed in one of three ways. By looking at the house from the outside you could tell how the inside was laid out. From babysitting, I found out that, regardless of outside similarities, a house had its own smells and energy (though I didn't know that word at the time).

Besides feeling different, each house was decorated to suit the owners. I saw possessions that my parents would not have dreamed of having: a picture of President Kennedy; a crucifix; a liquor cabinet. And where were the neighbors' books, which were found in every room of my family's house? I assumed their bookcases were in the rooms I did not enter.

I went home and thought about what I had seen and felt in the homes where I babysat. While the smells, sounds, and feelings of home comforted me, I didn't mind having questions. Why did each house feel so different? Why were some people Republicans and others Democrats? Why did my parents tell me that drinking made people miserable when that didn't seem to be true? My family was Baptist and Christian. Were Catholics Christians too? Why didn't more people read? Did they know what they were missing?

> **Babysitting Lesson #6: Career can take you out of your comfort zone—and that's a good thing!**

I figured I would babysit every summer until college. But when I was fifteen, my best friend Donna asked if I wanted to work with her at a peach orchard picking peaches—for $1.65 per hour. I quickly told my new client that, unfortunately, I could not babysit for her after all. I had a new career.

> **Babysitting Lesson #7: Changing careers can be easy.**

The Fields of California

Donna and I picked peaches in 100-degree Sacramento Valley heat. We picked the fruit the mechanized peach harvester did not shake out of the tree, the peaches still on the top branches. I don't remember getting scratched or bruised, though I must have. I only remember the sublime, fresh-from-the-tree taste of the peaches and their sweet, pungent smell.

After three days in the orchard, Donna and I were invited to join the crew at the sorting belt. Saying yes was the only answer. Not only was the work easier than picking, but we would work in an open-air covered shed—out of the sun.

The first day, I nervously took my place behind the conveyor belt. On one end of the belt came the peaches, straight from the field—maybe even the ones that Donna and I had picked the day before. On the other end, an empty bin waited like an open, hungry mouth. When full, it would be loaded on a truck and driven to the cannery. As the peaches passed on the moving belt, the sorters removed the peaches that were too green, too small, or too ripe to pass the cannery inspection.

The belt moved quickly; a sorter's eyes and hands had to move quickly as well. If a cannery inspector rejected a bin, the rancher blamed the sorting boss, who in turn blamed the crew.

Sorting peaches for six, eight, or ten hours a day was harder than reading kids to sleep and raiding cupboards, but I liked it. Jose, the boss, had sharp eyes and was quick to fire anyone who could not keep up. But he was also fair, laughed more than he yelled, and sometimes took Donna and me out for Mexican food after a shift.

The summer before I left that small town for college, I found a job that paid double what I earned in peaches: sorting tomatoes. Friends of friends honked outside my house at 5 A.M., followed by a twenty-mile drive to the tomato fields in the next county. Once there, I jumped on a tomato harvester, any one that had room for another worker.

Instead of working in a sorting shed, tomato sorters stood on the platform of the harvester as it moved through the fields ripping tomatoes from the vines. Along with tomatoes, the harvester also pulled up dirt clods triple the size of grapefruits and the occasional snake.

We sorted quickly, but were slowed by the clods and by the dirt in our eyes, nose, and mouth. Even with a face handkerchief covering everything but the eyes, I went home with dirt-packed nostrils as well as bruised hands, aching shoulders, and tired feet. But I stuck with it and proved to myself that I was not afraid of a little dirt.

When I look back at working in the fields now, I see that even though I wasn't babysitting anymore, I was using the same lessons. The dirt, snakes, and heat of the tomato fields didn't deter me; I still thought work was fun. It was fun to prove myself against myself, and to win.

> Babysitting Lesson #2: Work can be fun!

New York, New York

Thirty years after sorting tomatoes, I consulted for New York City mega-firms. The clients who needed my expertise leading software projects were world-class companies. Most of these companies employed more people than lived in my hometown.

Even in the City's slowdown of 2001, I enjoyed a thriving consultancy business, professional accolades, and a penthouse apartment overlooking the Hudson River. While I had vague thoughts about leaving project management someday, they were dreams and not plans. Why should I leave? I was fifty-one and in the top one percent of U.S. female wage earners. I could not fathom starting from scratch again.

Besides, I knew what it was like to start a career when others my age were fine-tuning theirs. I had left my first career, social work, at thirty. I walked away before I knew what I was going to do next. For eight years, I circled and turned, and supported myself in ways guaranteed not to make the graduate school newsletter: newspaper delivery driver, housecleaner, temporary office worker, waitress…. I even worked at McDonald's for two weeks, a job that delivers the extended version of "humility." (See Appendix A for the complete list of my jobs.)

For the most part, I didn't mind. The jobs supported me while I first figured out what career to pursue and also when I returned to school. Journalism school was fun and led to a job as a technical writer. But after six months of writing manuals, I was bored. I longed to exercise my mind in ways I never had before.

And so I returned to school again, this time in computer programming. One year later, computer programming became the entry point to a nearly twenty-year career in Information Technology.

No job was a waste; I learned about the beauty of Oakland, California, from delivering telephone directories there. But the software business was more rewarding. By taking more technical classes at night and honing my strengths, I quickly moved from programming to managing small projects, which in turn led to managing large projects. Eventually, I developed a specialty within project management: setting up procedures to more effectively deliver software projects.

In the beginning and through the middle, I enjoyed my career. I read everything I could, took classes, found a mentor, wrote articles, spoke at conferences, and threw myself into a leadership role in the leading professional association. And all the while I consulted for Fortune 100 companies on long-term assignments.

But gradually, my career passion waned. Still, I assumed project management would be the career blanket I would carry until "someday" arrived. Someday, I would have more autonomy at work. Someday, work would be more flexible. Someday, I would get paid for work that more clearly made a difference in the world. Someday....

Then, one October day in 2004, I did what I never thought would happen: I cried at work. I was at my desk in an open, everyone-can-see-everyone environment. And, not only were tears streaming down my face, but I was sobbing. Loudly.

My client at the time was an aggressive brokerage firm. I had just returned to my desk from a meeting with my temperamental boss. And while our exchange might have tipped the tears, I don't attribute them to him. The crying came from a deeper place.

As I cried, people looked at me and then looked away. Finally, one team member came over, gave me a tissue, and took charge. "Let's go to the ladies room," she said. I followed; I will never forget her kindness.

At the time I, of course, knew the rules. Rule #1: Don't cry at work. Rule #2: If you break Rule #1, don't let anyone see you.

But worst of all, for years I had forgotten—like an amnesia victim who forgets her identity—the most important babysitting lesson of all:

> Babysitting Lesson #2: Work can be fun!

In three months, the assignment at the brokerage firm ended. I vowed that the next client would be different: no mercurial boss for one thing, more meaningful work for another. Both happened. But still three questions lingered, ones that had surfaced in the space created by my crying jag. They were:

- ✦ What do I really want to do to make a living?
- ✦ What is holding me back?
- ✦ How can I make changes in a stress-free way?

Those are the questions that I answered over the next three years, as my career, once again, morphed into something new.

To make my journey into a map for you, let's start with the same questions:

+ What do you really want to do to make a living?
+ What is holding you back?
+ How can you make changes in a stress-free way?

To answer, let's move on to the three career myths. Is one of these myths holding you back from exploring your options?

2:
Career Myths

Myth #1: If you do what you love, the money will follow.

Almost twenty years ago, a book called *Do What You Love, the Money Will Follow* was published. What a great title! The book became a bestseller, and the title turned into a myth.

If you do what you love, maybe the money will follow, maybe it won't. It depends on you and the market's willingness to pay for what you love.

If you decide to follow your dream, I want the odds to be *high* that the money, in whatever amount you want, will follow. When embarking on a new venture, none of us can one hundred percent guarantee success. However, we can increase our odds through:

- ✦ Intending success
- ✦ Setting clear-cut goals
- ✦ Planning the steps to reach the goals
- ✦ Taking action
- ✦ Learning from others who have succeeded
- ✦ Assessing and revising our thoughts and actions

♦ *Becoming the person who can succeed*

Developing a fulfilling career isn't simplistic, nor is it destined for only a select few. It is a learned skill that anyone who truly wants to can learn. I hope that person is you.

Myth #2: Your passion and your career must match.

I can hear you now saying, "Huh? What? Your passion and your career must match is a *myth*? Haven't you been talking about having a fulfilling career all through the Introduction?"

Yes, I have, and that's what this book is about—achieving a fulfilling career. But who's to say that you should have only one passion, and that one passion should equal your career? Certainly not me! I hope you have multiple passions, the more the merrier. And if your career is one of them, great.

There's also the matter of timing. You might be in waiting mode for a fulfilling career. In the meanwhile, you're supporting yourself (and probably others) with "just a job." Does that make you a loser? Someone void of passion? Absolutely not!

I spent eight years between my first and second career. And even when I entered my second career, it took another four years to get to the part that I found truly exciting. During those years, I explored and developed activities and interests that enthralled me—after work hours. Was my work fulfilling? For the most part, no. Was my life passionate? Yes, even as I was making tons of career-change mistakes that I don't want you to make.

I'm relieved to be at the point in my life where career and passion go more closely together. It's my time, as my crying jag at my corporate job showed me. But to pin all your hopes and passions upon your career is like expecting one person to be everything for you—sexual partner, best friend, business partner, one-who-makes-you-laugh, and oh, what about fixing the leaky faucet?

Myth #3: A fulfilling career alone will make you happy.

A fulfilling career can help you to be happier. It can give you an outlet for expressing the beauty of you. But a fulfilling career, in and of itself, is just part of who you are. Career is only one way in which you spend your time, even if it's your biggest chunk. You have other layers to you. My wish is that you're happy and fulfilled in many areas—career, relationships, spirituality, fun, health, money.

This book starts with recognizing that you are a whole person. Your career self is just one part of you. As a result, we'll talk about more than your skills and past jobs. We'll explore you by digging deeper into who you are. Once you're ready, you can see how to align your true self to your earning-a-living self.

In all this digging, you'll uncover more than just a potential career. You'll discover the deeper you.

But first, let's peek to make sure career is what you want to change right now.

3:
Is it Time for a Career Change?

Sometimes when I mentor a woman in career change I find out, usually in the first session, that she wants a fulfilling relationship more than a fulfilling career. Before you go any further with this book, let's do a quick check to make sure that career is your culprit.

To do this, please rate how excited you are about these areas of your life, where ten means super-excited. Don't worry about how you're doing in these areas at the moment. Focus instead on how inspired, stimulated, or passionate you are, which is what I mean by "excited."

TABLE 3-1:

Area	Excitement Rating
Career	
Emotional Life *(quality of your thoughts and feelings & ability to express them to others)*	
Fun	
Friendships	

Health	
Money	
Relationship (as in emotional/sexual partnership)	
Spirituality (or Spiritual Practice)	

What did you find out? Were you surprised by any of your self-honest ratings? Where did career rate?

Interpret Your Score

Career doesn't have to rank at the bottom in order to work on it now. Nor must you limit your focus to one area of your life. In fact, if you're focusing on one area, other areas may improve or change for the better without any conscious effort on your part. I've especially seen that happen when I've made inner changes or discoveries.

(A digression here: I use the words "improve" and "change for the better" with caution. Sometimes, when outer circumstances seem just plain awful, inwardly we're grinding away and making soul-level changes in order to grow as a person. Do we hope and wish for these times? Not unless we're masochistic. Can we grow from them? Absolutely.)

To know whether now is the time for you to work on career, I'll ask you to do an intuitive assessment. After you completed your scoring, hold your finger over each category's rating for about thirty seconds. At the same time inwardly ask yourself, "Do I want to focus on this now?" Try to keep your thoughts as quiet as possible; this is an intuitive assessment. Your intuition doesn't speak from the mind.

After you've finished the first rating, continue to the next asking the same question until you finish. As you're doing this exercise, please don't think you'll have any insights or gain any conscious knowledge. Just do it for fun and forget about it.

Timing

If it's your time to do *something* about career, no matter how tiny or how huge, you'll do it. Or you won't and you'll suffer.

If it's *not* your time to focus on career, skip it. There are other areas for growth and development. Or you can focus on career change and suffer anyway.

It's all a matter of timing. Intuitively, you know whether this is your time to address career. If it is, keep reading and doing. Not only will you learn about career, you'll also learn how to quiet your mind so that your intuition can grow and guide you in big and small ways.

Let's start with the ugly: talking about what you don't like in your present career. Remember Allison from the Introduction? You'll meet her again in chapter 4.

4:
What Don't You Like?

Allison graduated from college four years ago and already wanted to change her career.

She had attended a prestigious university. When forced to pick a major, she chose marketing; it seemed as good as any of her other interests. After all, she thought, it would lead to a job, which she needed after graduation for rent, health insurance, and to pay off student loans.

In four years, Allison had had four jobs. Each time she left a job, she thought the next would prove that marketing really was for her. So far, that hadn't happened. She worried how future employers would judge her resume, but worried more about being miserable for eight hours a day.

"I still don't know what I want to do," she said. "My interests are varied—music and photography are only two. It's not like there's something that I can't wait to jump into. I have no clue how I could make money with what I like to do."

Allison wondered if she ever would.

Hating Your Job is a Gift

I told Allison, first of all, that hating her job was a gift.

"Because you are clear on what you don't like," I said, "it will be easier for you to discover what you do like."

I then asked Allison to spell out, in detail, what she didn't like about her job. As much as her job loathing was a gift, it was a gift she needed to leave behind; being miserable for eight-plus hours feels as bad as working all day in rain-soaked clothes. The sooner Allison could transform the energy of "I hate it" to the energy of "But there is something else I do like," the better she would feel.

To help Allison, I asked her what she didn't like about her job in these categories:

+ Physical environment where she works
+ Work hours
+ Commute
+ Business travel (this may or may not apply to you)
+ Office politics
+ Corporate style (such as flexible vs. structured)
+ Boss
+ Pay
+ Co-Workers and/or customers
+ The day-to-day tasks performed; the work itself
+ End product or service created by the company

As we went through the list, Allison had few complaints. It was not until I asked her about her boss that she winced, and said, "Nothing that I do is good enough for her. Even when I do something almost perfectly, she will find the smallest mistake to criticize. On top of that, she asks me to stay late and work, always at the last minute. And she assumes that I will say yes."

> Babysitting Lesson #4: Bosses can sometimes be unfair.

I listened, thinking that Allison might be more in need of mentoring on how to manage up than a career change. But then I asked her about her co-workers.

She said, "In all my marketing jobs, I have never found anyone that I felt comfortable with. This one is no different. I feel like a fish out of water."

Allison's words were a red flag. In careers that are a fit, we generally find people with whom we feel a bond. They don't have to turn into our best friends outside of work, but they should not seem like another breed.

When I asked her about the work itself, she was even more revealing. "Marina, what I do leaves me with a 'so what?' feeling. Even when I accomplish something, what does it matter that another sales campaign kicks off? Who cares? I guess, ultimately, the consumer benefits by buying a superior product. That's the theory anyway. But even if it's true, it's too thin a satisfaction to motivate and interest me. Way too thin."

The Opposite of What You Don't Like

Once Allison said what she didn't like, I asked her for the opposite. If her next career were the opposite of her current career, what would it look like?

But this time I asked Allison to take a few days and write down the opposite. Even if she talked it over with a friend first and then wrote, I wanted her to see *what she wanted* in print. There is power in the written word.

When Allison returned, she had written that her next career would be:

+ A career that I enjoy and that contributes to something that I believe in

+ Co-workers who could possibly be my friends

You can see that Allison was still vague; she didn't know *the* career that would make her forever, every-moment happy (which, by the way, doesn't exist). But she did know that:

+ She didn't hate *everything* about her job. From this, she realized that she hadn't flunked the select-a-job exam after all.

+ The things that she did *not* like were important to a healthy career. This compelled her to continue discovering a new career.

Alternatives to a Career Change

Like Rachel in the Introduction, you may not dislike your current career or job—but there is some change you would like to see happen or you would not continue with this book. It is important to recognize, specifically, what you want to be different so that the size of your solution fits the problem. Why vacuum the whole house when a spot-clean will do?

When you pinpoint what you would like to be different, you could find that less drastic changes are required. Instead of a wholesale career change you might:

+ **Change work hours or locations**—Working from home might be what you are really after. According to the U.S. Bureau of Labor Statistics[5], about fifteen percent of women work from home. Other surveys show that roughly double that percentage would like to.

+ **Change bosses**—According to Gallup research[6], a person's relationship with her immediate manager is the most important determinant of how long she stays and how productive she is at a job. Do you need a change of manager rather than a career change?

+ **Change companies**—Not all employers are alike. Corporate cultures vary dramatically, which is why lists of the "Best Companies to Work For" stay popular.

+ **Change industries**—Do you abhor working for a manufacturing company but would love the same position for a green company? Are you a teacher tired of squirmy kids who instead would like to train squirmy adults?

+ **Change what you do after work**—and focus on your passion. There are attorneys who sing in polka bands on the weekends, engineers who are models, and hair stylists who are authors. Why not you?

If you suspect you might want less than a wholesale career change, the system described in this book works for you, too. While you might need to customize the language slightly to accommodate your change, the principles are the same.

---

5 U.S. Bureau of Labor Statistics Work at Home Summary, 2005
6 *First, Break All the Rules: What the World's Greatest Managers Do Differently* by Marcus Buckingham and Curt Coffman

When the Mind is Foggy

The answer to the question, "Why do I want to change my career?" can be profound. Maybe you are gradually shifting your inner priorities or moving from one major phase of life to another. When change occurs, we often resist it more than welcome it—especially if the change seems imposed from the outside, like being laid off or fired.

These days, if deciding what to wear is hard for you, making career choices may be even harder. Don't worry. As you continue reading, your clarity will increase.

Besides, there was once someone else who was very, very unclear—me.

Stepping Stones to Clarity

As I mentioned in the Introduction, my first career was social work. My first job in that field, which began two weeks after I graduated from college and one week after getting married, was as a caseworker for families receiving public assistance.

In the beginning I loved what I did. But after a year, putting my finger in the dam of poverty began to hurt. In retrospect, I realize that casework met one of my core values, which was making a contribution. But working in a highly regulated bureaucracy stifled other values, such as achieving results and having flexibility.

In contrast, my then-husband, who was in medical school, must have had all of his values met, and more. He practically skipped to the hospital! He loved his work! And most impressive to both of our families, he was going to be a public health doctor and help tons of people!

I grew more and more discontented with social work. I didn't ask why I was so dissatisfied; I did not dissect my aversion. Instead, I decided to upgrade. In order to more efficiently solve societal problems (I talked like that at the time), I would become a lawyer, a class action attorney. As an attorney, I reasoned, I could also enjoy more flexibility and recognition.

The decision to become a lawyer came from my head. It was logical; it made sense.

When friends asked me why I was switching, I talked about lawyers who made a difference, like my heroes at the Southern Poverty Law Center. But the words were hollow; a part of me knew that my heart hadn't initiated this plan.

The application process began. I barely studied for the Law School Admission Test (LSAT), yet applied only to prestigious schools that required high LSAT scores. Now I see that my lack of preparation reflected my lack of even a spark of passion. At the time, I was oblivious. "Of course I want to be a lawyer," I told my husband when he compared my scant study time to the hours he had spent prepping for medical school admission tests.

Obliviousness ended after receiving the third and final rejection letter. My ego sobbed her eyes out while a more knowing part of me was relieved. Whew—one less thing that I didn't want to do. The rejection hurt too much for me to call it fortunate, but that is the word I use today.

After the rejection, I went to graduate school in another branch of social work, community organizing, and eventually worked in West Oakland organizing the first farmers' market in a California inner city. The job was the package I had been looking for years before: contribution, action, flexibility, and, yes, even recognition. Until one of my values shifted, it was perfect.

Chapter 4 Exercises

The Opposite Of

1. Answer the same questions about your career as Allison, the Marketing major, did. Why do you want to leave? What don't you like about your job or career? (If you're not currently working or working in your field, use the last job you held.) You can either write your answers or tell a friend.

2. Now, write or tell a friend the *opposite* of each item you do not like.

3. Notice your energy level as you write or talk. What depresses you or makes you the angriest about your dislike list? What inspires you the most about the opposite list?

Tell a Friend

1. Picture the face of your best friend, someone who has supported you time and time again.

2. Now, tell this person why you want to make a career move. They will listen to you without saying anything in reply. This is especially easy since they are not really there! Don't let your mind inhibit what you say; it will try.

3. Imagine that they ask you to repeat your reasons for changing your career. Reach deeper inside of yourself. Tell them again why you are changing careers. See what you tell them the second time.

4. How do you feel about your motivation for career change? Does it resonate with you?

5. Don't worry if you don't feel solid with your reasons. It's still early on.

Chapter 4 Summary

Congratulations! You have faced what you don't like about your current career. You have also looked at the opposite of your dislikes, that is, what you want in your next career. If a career shift seems too drastic, there are alternatives.

Most importantly, you have begun asking yourself, "Why do I want to make a career change?" The answer may not be clear yet, but it will be.

***

In the next chapter you'll meet Carmen, who knew why she switched careers—only her move did not turn out as expected.

5:
Self-Discovery

Carmen, in her mid-forties, was an accountant. She had become one on her parents' advice; they thought it was a "secure" profession. Over the years, she wished she were securely doing something else.

Then Carmen discovered jewelry: not jewelry-buying but jewelry-making. She sketched designs during her train commute to work, at unproductive meetings, and on the weekends. She then made what she sketched and wore her big, bold jewelry to her conservative workplace. She felt wild and out of place.

Eventually, Carmen quit her accounting job and began a jewelry company. With the back-up of a savings account, she designed, crafted, and marketed her own line.

Four years later, Carmen's savings were drying up. The jewelry sold but not enough to support her, even in a stripped-down style. Equally disturbing, Carmen said she was unhappy with what she did. When we met over coffee, she told me, "I thought jewelry was my passion, but I'm already bored and overworked at the same time. I'm not sure this was the right decision."

Understandably, Carmen was skittish about switching careers again.

Avoiding the Quick Fix

Carmen knew I wasn't a quick-fix mentor. Still, she rebelled when I asked her to spend one week discovering, not her options, but herself.

"I've read more self-help books than Tony Robbins," she told me. "And don't get me started on personal development courses. I've been to them all."

I laughed. "That's great," I told her. "I'm not asking you to read a book or take a course. All you need to do is to take a quiz—but in a leisurely way, a stress-free way. Maybe there are still a few things that you don't know about yourself, clues that will help with your career."

Carmen agreed, though she was still skeptical that she would find anything new.

"Who Are You?" Questionnaire

I gave Carmen my "Who Are You?" questionnaire, and asked her to take the entire week to complete it. I told her to fill out the answers only when she felt relaxed. But before she answered, she had to visualize that she was a tree in spring whose buds were just opening up.

Carmen groaned, and then saw that I was just teasing about the visualization. But I wasn't teasing when I asked her *not* to connect any answers with career ideas. "If career ideas pop into your head," I told her, "write them down in a journal. Then forget about them."

The questions Carmen completed were from three different time periods of her life. I won't give you her answers, but will let you discover your own.

Childhood

1. As a child, how did you spend your free time? What did you do that caused you to lose track of time?

2. When people asked you what you wanted to do when you grew up, what did you say? Did you say different things at different ages? Why did you mention the careers you did? Would you say the same thing now?

3. Who were your childhood heroines or heroes? Name three, and say why.

4. What types of books, games, or movies captivated your attention? How did this change during your childhood?

Teenager or Young Adult

1. What were your first jobs outside of the home? What did you learn? How did you feel about working?

2. If you attended college or vocational school, what led to your choosing your course of study? On a scale of 1 to 4, with 4 being the most passionate, how passionate were you about your major?

Present

1. If your career has changed before, how would you describe your career change? (Your change may include moving from student to worker.)

2. If you could wave a magic wand and change every single person on the planet in one way, how would

you change us? Does the change with your magic wand relate to one of your passions?

3. What is one positive trait, quality, or characteristic about yourself that hardly anyone knows?

4. On your deathbed, what is the one phrase you want to say that will encapsulate your life?

Self-Discovery Assessments

In a week, Carmen returned. She was embarrassed to admit that she wanted more self-discovery time; she asked for another two weeks.

"Of course," I told her. "Go at your own pace." I directed her to the resources in Appendix B, some of which are closely linked with career. But her instructions were the same: she wasn't to research or even think about career possibilities. She was to focus on herself.

In two weeks, she bubbled with excitement. "I know why jewelry making seems boring to me! And the reason has nothing to do with my creativity. I'm not losing my creative touch."

I looked at Carmen with surprise. I hadn't realized that she, who dripped with creativity, had any doubts about her talent.

Carmen reminded me that she had turned to jewelry while in the deepest hole of her accounting career. Her designs represented freedom; they were a way out of her left-brain prison. But when she started the business, Carmen entered the reality of the jewelry business: finding material, sales outlets, and buyers; creating publicity and buzz; deciding what trade shows to attend; building a website; and learning online marketing.

She had wanted to create jewelry, not a business.

Carmen said that by focusing on herself for three weeks, without the pressure of coming up with a new career idea, she had seen that she linked jewelry with creativity in her mind. "If jewelry equals creativity for me, then leaving the jewelry business meant I was not creative, which is absolutely not true!" Carmen said this with the surety of a new convert—a convert to discovering herself.

Mind Clicks

Author Dr. Robert Cialdini writes about, in his book *The Psychology of Persuasion*, what he calls "click-whirr responses." I call these "mind clicks." Mind clicks are short-cuts our brains take to make decisions. For example, if an expert or celebrity endorses a product, we are more apt to buy it; our automatic response equates an endorsement with the thought, "This might be good for me, too." If a non-profit sends us free address labels, the "mind click" is, "They did something for me; I should reciprocate." (If you think you don't fall for these marketing mind clicks, test yourself by reading Cialdini's book.)

Mind clicks can save us decision-making time, especially in this Information-Overload Age. But they can also limit or stop change. When Carmen unconsciously associated jewelry with creativity, she nearly convinced herself that if she no longer created jewelry, she could not be creative. The hidden association in her mind prevented her from seeing her options.

The Downside of Experience

The older we are, the more experience we have to draw upon. And the older we are, the more mind clicks we have encoded. What if a forty-five-year-old's aversion to failure were embedded inside the brain of a one-year-old learning to walk? The poor kid would give up after two tries.

As we become aware of the shortcuts our minds make, we can avoid them.

Discovering a Mind Click

During my project management career, I was offered a business opportunity that I couldn't pass up: partnership in a fledgling technology placement company. I loved working for myself; I discovered my entrepreneurial spirit. I also liked our success. In less than two years, we profitably sold the company.

> Babysitting Lesson #3: Having money is great!

Self-discovery aside, the two years had not been a picnic. In the beginning, we did everything ourselves, from cold calling to interviewing candidates to typing resumes. I consistently worked eighty hours a week. Worse, I did and thought of little else but the start-up business; I poured all of my energy into it.

Years later, when I began the search for a passionate third career, I thought about starting my own business again. But I was ten years older, with more interests than just business. My "mind click" quickly screamed, "No way am I going to work eighty hours a week again and tie myself to a business! Forget it!"

So I did.

It wasn't until I continued shining the flashlight on myself—and sometimes giving the flashlight to skilled friends and mentors—that I saw the association I had fused together in my mind. *Start-up business* equaled *all work, no fun* to me.

By seeing my "mind click", I was able to break it.

I again started a new business, for I am an entrepreneur at heart. Equally important, I do not work eighty hours a week: I do have a life outside of work.

Chapter 5 Exercises

Who Are You?

1. Take the Who Are You? Questionnaire in this chapter or at www.pinkedge.com in the "free stuff" section.

2. Visit the online assessment websites listed Appendix B and take the quizzes that appeal to you. Many are free.

3. Write in a journal or tell a friend what surprises you had when completing #1 and #2 above.

Catching "Mind Clicks"

1. Most people are able to list the career mind clicks of their best friend while failing to see them in themselves. Give it a try anyway. What are three of your mind clicks that relate to your career change? If this is difficult, you can pretend to be someone else who is analyzing you.

2. Tell someone you trust about your mind clicks as they relate to career. Examples might be that you equate "long hours" with "deserve recognition," or "appreciation from boss" to "self-worth." Ask them what they think of your mind clicks, and then listen to their responses without agreeing or disagreeing.

Chapter 5 Summary

Three cheers! You are leisurely continuing your discovery with an assessment of who you are—now. If you chose to, you took other quizzes that helped you to explore your values, personality, and skills. You became more aware of mind clicks and how they affect you.

***

In the next chapter, we will deepen our discovery with an ancient technique that is still fresh and vital.

6:
Tuning In

Rachel, in her fifties, worked for the state government for the past twenty-five years. Through those years, she saw her department—which she now headed—grow in size, maturity, and customer responsiveness. She was proud that jokes about non-caring, unmotivated government employees were not true of the 250 people who worked under her. Rachel was efficient and personable. She was demanding, yet her employees felt cared for and respected.

While Rachel was good at her job, which was satisfying, she also wondered if she was limiting herself. She toyed with the idea of quitting to start a business, but that didn't make economic sense when she was so close to retirement. Still, the thought of another eight years doing something that she liked—but that no longer challenged her—was about as appealing as cold oatmeal. She wasn't married and had no children. "I have nothing to tie me down," she thought. "What do I want to do with my life?"

Rachel's quandary cleared when I taught her how to tune in.

Powerful First Inner Key

Tuning in is a technique modified from meditation, a practice mentioned in nearly every book and article about stress management. On television, Dr. Mehmet Oz, Oprah's on-show physician, declared meditation to be the #1 stress-buster.

The beneficial results of meditation are documented by scientific evidence. One study, conducted by Jon Kabat-Zinn, Ph.D., showed that people who meditate shift their brain activity from the stress-prone right frontal cortex to the calmer left frontal cortex, thereby decreasing the negative effects of stress, mild depression, and anxiety.

What cannot be scientifically proven—yet—is meditation's ability to access your untapped powers. Leaving your powers untapped is like walking barefoot on hot concrete when shoes are readily available: you can do it, but it causes unnecessary pain.

Untapped Powers

Even if you don't like the cold, please humor me and think of yourself as an iceberg. While the numbers vary depending on the iceberg, roughly ninety percent of an iceberg's mass is submerged and only ten percent revealed, above the water line.

Now, think of your conscious thoughts and behaviors as the tip of the iceberg. We think of this tip as our personality, as us. In that small portion are crammed likes and dislikes, memories and future dreams, and endless commentary. Quite a lot for a small space!

Now imagine the largest portion, the ninety percent. This huge part is our subconscious mind. This isn't the subconscious that Freud talked about, but a vast part of us that isn't under the control of the conscious mind. You might think of it as your awareness.

Subconscious Mind

I divide the subconscious—the large, submerged part of the iceberg—into three sections. Why? It just helps me to remember all that's there, that's why.

One part stores characteristics that, when they first break free of conditioning, surprise the conscious mind. For example, I grew up in an extremely religious Christian family. In my family, holding oneself back so that someone else could win, whether it was a game, an argument, or the attention, was considered a virtue. My conscious mind, the small tip of my iceberg, was shocked when I first broke free from this familial programming and realized that winning invigorated me. Who knew?

Another section of the subconscious mind houses intuition, hunches, and instincts. This is the information that we receive outside of the medium of the five senses. Generally, women are more apt to listen to this information and, as a result, trust it and allow the access to grow. (Intuition is such an important aid in your career journey that we will cover it more completely in chapter 14.)

The third section of our subconscious is our spirit, our essence. You might prefer to call it your deeper self, higher power, or your soul. In the rest of this book, you will often hear me refer to it as your inner self. It is the place where God, the Divine, the Universe—whichever name you like—dwells. The power of this part of you cannot be underestimated, just as the power of a hurricane should not be.

How to Tune In

You may already have a way in which you access your inner self. Since the Self speaks the language of silence, my recommendation is to begin by quieting the thoughts that reside in the tip of the iceberg — you know, the thoughts in your mind that think they run the show.

Every day, around sixty thousand thoughts race through our minds (a statistic I learned from Jack Canfield, co-author of the *Chicken Soup for the Soul* series). Too often, they are boring, petty, or self-defeating. They definitely repeat themselves. There are many ways to quiet them so that you can tune in to your inner nature. When you do, you will find the best career coach you can ever imagine.

Heart-Focused Tuning In

1. Go to your favorite spot in your house or apartment—the area where you feel the most relaxed (other than the bathroom). Once there, sit in a chair, sofa, or on a cushion on the floor, whatever is the most comfortable for you. If you prefer, play soothing music in the background (but no television or radio).

2. Close your eyes, sit as straight as you can, and point to your heart area as if you were saying "me." This is the area on which you will focus. I will call it the heart center. Focus on that whole area, not on the heart organ itself.

3. Slowly pay attention to your heart center. Focus on it, meaning put your mental attention there. Then feel it, as if you were feeling it from the inside out. If you

wish, you can follow your breath as it moves in and out of your heart center.

4. Ignore any thoughts you have, for you will have many. When you notice yourself thinking, return to focusing.

5. Continue this focus for five to ten minutes. (Bringing a clock or watch with you to your spot is okay.) In the beginning, don't go longer than ten minutes; five minutes is perfectly fine in the beginning.

6. When finished, smile—big. Ear to ear. Show teeth. Hold the smile for as long as you can. One minute? Two? Longer? You may feel silly, and that is allowed.

7. Congratulations! If tuning in is new to you, you have taken an important step to boost your ability to connect with your deeper self. Even if you were able to focus for only one-eighth of a nanosecond, you are learning to draw power from the source.

Why does Tuning In Work?

Tuning in works for several reasons. Tuning in makes us feel better because thoughts can be tiring and draining. Washing them out is like giving our mind a shower. By tuning in, we slow down and ultimately silence the mind. Fortunately, even a tiny, partial slowdown can feel refreshing.

Tuning in also works because we focus on the heart, which is the center of love, compassion, and beauty. By focusing on it, you are activating the energy in that area and strengthening your capacity for what resides there—love, compassion, and beauty.

It is my guess that those capacities consciously or subconsciously motivated you to begin your new career journey. Aren't you showing love and compassion for yourself by searching to find your passion? Aren't you looking for the place in the world that you can really make a difference? Aren't you looking for a way to express your beauty and find those who will appreciate it?

While tuning in, you are strengthening these fundamental, motivating feelings.

Most importantly, tuning in works to access the untapped power of the deeper self—the soul—because silence is the language of the soul. Our inner self is our bridge to God, and words are too slow and clumsy a medium to connect with such a force. By quieting our minds, we can learn to listen.

I realize this all might sound pie-in-the-sky—until you experience it yourself through tuning in.

Beginning

Rachel, the government manager, looked at me in surprise when I suggested that she practice the tuning-in exercise every day for ten minutes. "I don't have time!" she exclaimed.

"It seems paradoxical, but this will actually give you more time," I explained. "You've already told me that because you're bored, you watch too much TV."

Rachel nodded in agreement, perhaps regretting that she had told me that piece of information.

"So, try this for a week and see how you feel at the end," I said. "It can be a trial week. If you don't like it, you can skip it; but, first, what about giving it a real try? Suspend your disbelief for one week."

She agreed. Next, we talked about the best time of the day to tune in. I told her that first thing in the morning, after her coffee or tea, was best.

"I'm not a morning person!" she said, "There is no way that I can get up even fifteen minutes earlier."

Rachel did commit to an evening time, before she was too sleepy to focus but after she had wound down from work.

Here are the additional tips that I gave to Rachel:

1. Tune in somewhere in your house or apartment where you have privacy, even from your spouse or partner. If you want, you can put flowers or a beautiful picture in that spot.

2. Turn off your cell phone during that time. Unplug any other devices that might disturb you.

3. Wear comfortable clothing; you want to be able to breathe.

4. When focusing on your heart center, think of nothing but two things: your focus on your heart center and your breath. Unlike the rest of the day, you are doing something one-pointedly.

5. If any thoughts come up that are not related to your focus (and they will), ignore them and go back to focusing. Notice and go back. Notice and go back. That will happen time and time again.

6. Unless you are accustomed to practicing something similar to tuning in, do not exceed ten minutes. You can always increase your time later.

Alternative Methods

Rachel took to tuning in like a Labrador to water. After only a week, she said she had more energy and what she called freshness about her future. She especially liked being forced to smile, and found that, after a few days, smiling came naturally. She also said she caught herself smiling more at work.

I taught Rachel and Carmen, the accountant-turned-jewelry designer, the tuning-in technique at the same time. Carmen was enthusiastic but surprised herself by not being able to sit still. "Marina, I try," she told me. "But I want to get up and scream after only a few minutes. I don't like closing my eyes. I feel claustrophobic."

I asked her what she did that helped her to feel more relaxed.

"Sketching," she replied. "When I sketch, I feel like my worries go away."

Carmen and I then designed a tune-in method around sketching. Like Rachel, she tried it as an experiment for a week. Carmen sketched first thing in the morning. When she did, she noticed her thoughts and focused on what she was doing. When she drew, she drew. She noticed the feel of her arms as they moved and the sensation of the pen in her hand.

And, when she finished, she smiled, the big-grin smile.

If you feel more comfortable working your way up to the tuning—in exercise, consider an alternative done in the focused way that Carmen sketches:

- ✦ Painting, sculpting, or pottery
- ✦ Yoga or stretching
- ✦ Tai Chi

- ✦ Dancing
- ✦ Listening to music
- ✦ Walking, especially in nature
- ✦ Gardening
- ✦ Praying (if it is about the connection and not about what you want)
- ✦ Chanting
- ✦ Tea ceremony
- ✦ Flower arranging
- ✦ Guided visualizations (but not visualizations of yourself achieving your goals or in a future state: they are too mental)
- ✦ Writing without editing or censoring

Complements to Tuning In

Tuning in will soothe and open your soul. Two other activities in particular complement tuning in. The first is spending time in nature.

Nature teaches us much about silence. The more we go with the intention of being and listening, the more our experiences in nature can be tuning-in times. Beauty is all around; the emptier our minds are, the more we can see and feel it.

Working out is the second activity that complements tuning in. In addition to releasing endorphins that our brains like, exercise releases the negative energy that our energy bodies picked up during the day. When we finish working out, we feel more like ourselves and less like the people we have been around.

My First Tuning In

Rachel was more adept at tuning in than I.

Years ago, I stumbled across meditation, the root of tuning in, and thought I would give it a try. For some reason, I thought I would be good at it, for then I rarely tried anything if I thought I might fail. The method I learned was similar to the tune in exercise of this chapter.

The first morning, after coffee, I leaned my back against the living room couch and stretched my legs out in front of me. After years of running and not enough stretching, my legs wouldn't tolerate a cross-legged pose. With an alarm clock at my side, I closed my eyes and expected to plunge into the beautiful silence of my inner self.

All I heard was the cranky and chattering voice of me. For a millisecond I focused on my heart, then thoughts yanked me back to the important: the itch in my knee, what I would eat for breakfast, why I should be good at this, the movie last night....

After hearing at least twenty minutes of this chatter, I started to get up, hoping that it was all right to meditate longer than the suggested fifteen minutes the first time. But I checked the clock just in case. Two minutes!! What!! Only two minutes had gone by!!

I returned to trying to focus. When I finished, I was sure that I was wasting my time with this nonsense. But some part of me, definitely not the top-of-the-iceberg portion, wanted to meditate the next day. And the next. And the next. In a month, I became more accustomed to the rhythm of my mind and began experiencing spaces between the thoughts. These spaces helped me to gradually begin dipping into the deeper part of me.

I still cannot sit cross-legged for very long, but I have been meditating daily for more than twenty-five years.

Additional Tuning In Techniques: Breathing and Gazing

It's helpful to periodically change your tuning-in practice so that it doesn't become just another routine. As you'll see, the breathing technique below shares some steps with the heart-focused technique you learned earlier in the chapter.

Breathing Steps

1. Go to a relaxing spot in your house or apartment. Once there, sit in a chair, sofa, or on a cushion on the floor—whatever is comfortable.

2. Close your eyes, sit as straight as you can, and breathe. Yes, that's all that you need to do. Breathe. Follow your breath in and follow your breath out.

3. As you did with your heart center, focus on your breath. Put your mental attention there. Focus.

4. Ignore any thoughts you have, for you will have many. When you notice yourself thinking, return to focusing.

5. Continue focusing on your breath for five to ten minutes. (Bringing a clock or watch with you to your spot is okay.) In the beginning, don't go longer than ten minutes; five minutes is fine in the beginning.

6. When finished, smile—big. Ear to ear. Show teeth. Hold the smile for as long as you can. One minute? Two? Longer? You may feel silly, and that is allowed.

7. Congratulations! You're tuning in to the source.

Gazing Steps

You can also use gazing as a warm-up, in which case you would practice it for one to two minutes immediately before one of the other techniques.

1. Pick an object upon which you'll gaze. It could be a flower, a pretty rock, or the picture of a spiritual teacher who inspires you. If you're outside, you might choose a plant, flower, or leaf. It's easiest if the object on which you're gazing is about level with your eyes when you look straight ahead.

2. For this technique, keep your eyes open. Now, softly look at the object. Don't stare; blink when necessary. But focus. Put your mental attention on the object. Focus.

3. Ignore any thoughts you have, for you will have many. When you notice yourself thinking, return to focusing on the object.

4. Continue focusing on the object for five to ten minutes. At first, do not exceed ten minutes; five minutes is fine in the beginning.

5. When finished, smile—big. Ear to ear. Show teeth. Hold the smile for as long as you can. One minute? Two? Longer? You may feel silly, and that is allowed.

6. Congratulations! You're tuning in to the source.

Chapter 6 Exercises

Tuning In

1. If you are new to a method of quieting your thoughts each day, decide whether you will tune in for a week—as an experiment. If you decide not to, you might change your mind and come back to this chapter later on. Tuning in is the foundation of the stress-free way; I can't say enough about its benefits.

2. If you decide to tune in, choose your method. If you like, you can begin with one of the alternative methods and then move on to the heart-focused, breathing, or gazing technique.

3. Write in a journal or tell a friend about your experiences—either as you go along or at the end of the week. How was it? Was tuning in easier or harder than you thought it would be?

4. What questions do you have about tuning in? Feel free to email me at marina@pinkedge.com

Nature

✦ Take a walk in nature by yourself. If possible and if safe, walk where fewer people go. Walk with the intent of tuning in to yourself through nature.

✦ On your walk, focus on what you are seeing and feeling. How do your feet sound against the trail? How do you feel in your body? How does the wind feel against your face? What are you seeing that strikes you as beautiful? As unusual?

Working Out

✦ If you do not regularly work out, consider adding it to your repertoire. Depending upon your age and physical health, you may need to consult a health care professional before beginning.

✦ Start slowly. Begin in small doses until you develop both your muscles and the routine. I'm talking baby, baby steps—like buying walking shoes and just looking at them for a few days before you take your first step out the door.

✦ For most people, it helps being around others who are working out. Consider joining a woman-friendly gym where you are supported in your new habit.

✦ Take heart that, like bad habits, good habits are hard to break once they take hold.

Chapter 6 Summary

Amazing! You learned a beautiful technique for successfully continuing your new career journey—tuning in. It is a type of meditation, and the foundation of the stress-free way. By tuning in to your inner self, you are listening to the wisest part of you. You will meet the best career coach you have—you.

If tuning in through the sitting method is awkward at first, you have alternative approaches. In addition, you can complement tuning in with nature and exercise.

***

Now, with more insight to your inner self with tuning in, let's re-visit Allison as she meets Aunt Clara.

7:
What Would You Do Without Pay?

After learning to tune in, Allison felt less in need of rescue from her job; calmness seeped into her panic.

Allison had also taken the "Who Are You?" questionnaire as well as other assessments. She said she now knew more about herself than she ever had before—and she still did not know what career suited her best.

So I took Allison on a guided visualization. I learned the visualization from one of my mentors, Keith Cunningham, who teaches business classes for entrepreneurs. Though Keith calls the main character Uncle Ned, I renamed him Aunt Clara.

You can do the same visualization as Allison. One important fact to know about Aunt Clara is that she is a billionaire.

Aunt Clara's Legacy

With your eyes closed, pretend that you are the beloved niece of your billionaire aunt, Aunt Clara. Having no children of her own, Aunt Clara loves you the best among all the nieces and nephews.

But, sadly, Aunt Clara passes away. Hundreds of people come to the service, both to pay their respects and to silently speculate about the will. After the funeral service, Aunt

Clara's attorney asks you to meet with him privately. Wondering what he will say, you agree, and travel the short distance to his office.

In the office, you sit facing the attorney, who is behind a large oak desk. He opens a document, which is Aunt Clara's trust, and reads from it.

You can hardly believe what you are hearing. Aunt Clara has left you, her favorite niece, *all* of her fortune. You are set for life, rich beyond your wildest dreams!

The attorney says that there is one stipulation. "Of course," you think. "There is always a catch." You hold your breath.

The stipulation is that, in order to receive the fortune, you must continue to work every day. You do not have to work for someone else, nor do you have to earn money—you do not need the money. But you do need to work doing something.

"What work will you do?" the attorney asks.

Interpreting Aunt Clara

When you ask yourself the Aunt Clara question, be sure to catch the first images or thoughts that cross your mind after the question, "What work will you do?" It doesn't matter how illogical the pictures or words are, just notice them. Allison saw herself helping children in some way. But she was not sure of the setting or what exactly she was doing.

About ninety percent who have taken the Aunt Clara exercise have glimpsed career pictures, thoughts, or feelings when asked the final question. However, what pops into your mind might not make logical sense. For example, you might see scenes of you cooking or traveling and wonder what that has to do with work. Or you might know that you want to write but not know what about. Don't worry. We are still early on.

For the ten percent who experience a big blank with the visualization: have patience. If you continue tuning in and then return to Aunt Clara, you probably will have a different experience. The soul has its own time frame to reveal things to you; as you become more adept at listening, you will hear.

The Importance of Values

The beauty of the Aunt Clara exercise is that it allows you to separate what you would like to do from making money. By making the separation, you can imagine yourself doing work that suits your values rather than the rent or mortgage payment.

Our values, consciously or subconsciously, motivate us. When we most dislike what we are doing, we are not aligned with our values. For example, if one of your top values is honesty and you are in a job where you are expected to lie or cover up for your boss, you might be miserable.

While it's wonderful when work fulfills our values, career isn't the only vehicle. If family is one of your key values, it doesn't mean you have to schlep all your kids to work or work at home. Instead, it might mean that you choose a career that doesn't demand evening or weekend work, and preferably gives you some flexibility during the day.

In addition to the Aunt Clara visualization, other resources in Appendix B will help you to identify your current values, for they do shift.

Shifting Values

I mentioned that when I worked in West Oakland as a community organizer, the job gave me the value package I had been looking for—contribution to others, results, flexibility, and recognition. But eventually I left social work because one of my values shifted.

The value that shifted was contribution. I realized that, while I seemed to be making a contribution to other people, I needed to step back and give to me. This wasn't a sudden insight; it started with my separation and eventual divorce. From there, the need to look within kept percolating, like a pot of water coming to a boil. Questions just wouldn't go away. Who was I? Why did I do the things I did? Where was I headed?

At the time, I seemed incapable of discovering me and contributing to others full-time. Others, I knew, did it; I couldn't. With a smidgen of savings, I left social work to look for a career that would better support my questioning. I guessed that I might need some retraining, but figured that, in two years maximum, I would be back on the career track.

I did go back to school, twice. It took me eight years to find and kick off my new career in the computer field. As I like to say, I made every mistake in the book, whatever that book is.

If you'd like, let's make your career shift much shorter. That's not a problem; I'm here to help you learn from my mistakes. Aunt Clara would like to help as well.

Chapter 7 Exercises

1. Do the Aunt Clara exercise—at a time when you feel the most relaxed and still. This might be after you have tuned in, after a bubble bath, or when you return from a walk in nature. You can lead yourself through the visualization or have someone read it to you (preferred).

2. Write down or tell a friend what you would do if you worked without needing to work.

3. You may repeat this exercise as many times as you wish; your answers might change.

Chapter 7 Summary

You've done it again! By completing the Aunt Clara exercise, you are beginning to know what your heart wants to do. Your images may be vague but they are percolating. Congratulations!

***

In the next chapter, let's check in again with Allison, Carmen, and Rachel as they compare lifestyles and complete Discovery.

8:
Your Lifestyle

While Allison, Carmen, and Rachel began gentle searches for energetic role models, I asked them to consider how they wanted their careers to fit with their lives. "Sometimes it is even more important to support a vital lifestyle concern than to find the most fulfilling work," I said, thinking of how much I enjoyed working for myself—all except the long hours—when I owned the technology placement company. Technical recruiting was not a passion, but being an entrepreneur was.

I asked Allison, Carmen, and Rachel to slowly answer the following lifestyle questions. Since all three were tuning in, in their respective ways, I wanted them to feel out the answers, using their inner selves as guides.

Lifestyle Questionnaire

1. Where do you want to work? From home? A large corporation? A small office?

2. For whom do you want to work? Yourself? A manager who can help guide you? Within an organization, but one where you have more autonomy?

3. With whom do you want to work? No one? A large team? A small team? A few select people of your choice?

4. How structured do you want your work to be? Do you like predictability? Or do you thrive on chaos and constant change?

5. Do you want to travel on business? Not at all? Much of the time? Sometimes?

6. What appreciation or attention do you need from other people? Minimal? Lots? Somewhere in between? (Be real; answering this question might require a conversation with a friend willing to be direct with you.)

7. How much money do you need or want to earn? In the beginning? As time goes on?

> Babysitting Lesson #5: Get paid what you are worth.

Lifestyle Answers

Allison, who was just beginning her career, had only a few lifestyle requirements. She did not want to work at home and wanted to work with a team. These requirements fit with Allison's extroverted personality. She was relatively flexible about money, since her misery-producing jobs of the past four years had at least paid well. Her student loans had been pared down.

Carmen, who had worked for both a large corporation and for herself, was adamant that she would never again step foot in a Fortune 500 company—at least not as an employee. She loved working mostly at home, and would not consider another lifestyle.

While completing the Lifestyle questionnaire, Rachel, the government manager, saw that sticking with her current job until retirement—and starting a small business on the side—was the best choice for her. By allowing herself to explore other possibilities, she had satisfied her career curiosity. She also said that tuning in every day brought her the happiness she was trying to find in work, plus gave her more energy to start a side venture.

The Maybe List

Before they left the Discovery phase, I asked Allison, Carmen, and Rachel to decide, for now, whether they wanted to make a wholesale or partial career shift. I told them it wasn't like donating an organ (although it could be like finding their hearts); they could always change their minds.

Next, I asked them to make a list of the careers, businesses, or interests they wanted to explore further. I called this the Maybe List. The list would have potential ventures that resulted from the Discovery phase activities they did:

+ Asking "Why?"—why you want to change careers
+ Self-discovery—finding out who you are now
+ Tuning in—a gentle type of meditation
+ Aunt Clara—visualization that separates work from money
+ Guiding Star—"if she can do it, I can do it"
+ Lifestyle needs—requirements that a career will accommodate

Their Maybe Lists looked like this:

TABLE 8-1:

Allison	Goal
(recent college graduate who discovered she didn't hate everything about her job)	Definitely change career, maybe to: ✦ Psychologist ✦ Radio Announcer ✦ Teacher

Carmen	Goal
(corporate dropout who wanted to stay creative outside of a corporation)	Stay with jewelry but do it differently. Add another creative, money-making venture like: ✦ Illustrating children's books ✦ Storytelling ✦ Writing

Rachel	Goal
(government manager who wondered if she should be doing more with her life)	Stick with my job until retirement but start a side business—maybe: ✦ Selling on E-Bay ✦ Helping women with their careers ✦ Real estate

Chapter 8 Exercises

Lifestyle Questionnaire

1. Take a moment to fill out the Lifestyle questionnaire. It's also on <u>www.pinkedge.com</u> in the "free stuff" section.

2. Did any of your answers surprise you? What about the answers surprised you?

Maybe List

Now, complete your Maybe List. The two questions you will answer with your list are:

1. Do I want to completely change my career, or make a less dramatic shift? (If you want to make a dramatic shift, it does not mean you have to do it all at once.)

2. What are the Maybe options I want to explore further? (This will be done in the next phase, Zooming In.)

Checklist of the Discovery Phase

Some people love checklists and others loathe them. If this one brings up bad memories from school or work, skip it and move on to the Summary.

If you like checklists, use this to gauge what you did against activities in the Discovery phase.

❏ I have asked myself why I want to leave my career and what I don't like.

❏ I know whether I want to leave my career or make a less dramatic change.

❑ If I dislike my present job, I know specifically what I do not like about it.

❑ If I dislike my present job, I know the opposites of my dislikes.

❑ I have completed the Who Am I? questionnaire.

❑ I have completed _____ (fill in the number) of the online assessments from Appendix B.

❑ I have read _____ (fill in the number) of the resources in Appendix B.

❑ I am practicing tuning in, or an equivalent that works for me.

❑ I have done the Aunt Clara visualization.

❑ I have completed The Pink Edge Lifestyle questionnaire.

❑ I have at least two ideas of what I might do next.

Discovery Activities

See Figure 8-1 for Discovery Phase Activities

Chapter 8 Summary

Double congratulations! You have completed this chapter and the Discovery phase. You've considered your lifestyle requirements and how they might impact your career choice. You have also created a Maybe List of career options. You are ready to move on to Zooming In, where you will begin research on those options.

Discovery Phase Activities
Figure 8-1

PART 2
Zooming In

9:
Gathering Facts

Tania, a soon-to-be-divorced mother of two, graduated from the Discovery phase with two potential careers on her Maybe List: teaching kids and training adults in corporate settings. She was most drawn to teaching kids and even had an age group in mind—high school—but she didn't want to limit her options.

"That's great," I told her. "For people who are short on ideas, the Discovery phase helps you to expand your options. For those with a gazillion ideas, the same phase can help to pare down the choices. In this new phase, Zooming In, you will narrow your list by gathering facts. You'll become a researcher on your potential careers."

Tania loved the idea of gathering facts. When she had taken the Kolbe assessment, one of the resources in Appendix B, she discovered that she was strong in "fact finding." She overflowed with questions: What were the pros and cons of teaching versus training? If she chose teaching, what did she need to do to get a teacher's certificate? How long would it take? Most importantly, how much would it cost and where would she get the money?

She could not wait to dig into the answers.

Making Research Fun (or at Least Tolerable)

Not everyone is a fact finder; happily, we have diverse skills and different ways of approaching problems. If fact finding sounds as exciting as cutting toenails, start with what sounds the easiest from the following:

1. Read books on your topic that are written by authors who are successful doing what you want to do. For example, aspiring writers might read *Bird by Bird* by Anne Lamott or *Wild Mind: Living the Writer's Life* by Natalie Goldberg.

2. If your Maybe List has interests that do not fit neatly into a particular career, search the internet for sites that match your interest. For example, if scrapbooks are your passion but you don't know of a career as a "scrapbooker," use your favorite search engine, such as Google or Yahoo, for ideas. After typing the word in the search engine, what sites come up? What ideas do those sites give you? What do they *not* provide that you could? How is your vision unique?

3. Check out the people who are in the career that interests you. Observe, if even from a distance, what it's like to be in that career. An example: if you want to work on Wall Street or your city's equivalent, go there during lunch and walk around. Check out the people. What are they wearing? Would you feel comfortable in that "uniform"? Do you notice any similarities between the workers? Are the conversations you overhear what you want to be talking about? What about the "vibe" of the people? Of the area? Would you want to work there? Your answers

might surface on an intuitive level, which we'll cover in chapter 14.

4. A more traditional approach that I still recommend is to talk to at least three people who are doing what you want to do. You can take the structured or unstructured approach.

   a. Unstructured—Go to where your potential people are. Join the professional association or attend the conference in your new subject area. Casually strike up conversations, and then *listen* and *observe*. What do they like about their work? What are the complaints? The rewards? How does the energy feel to you? Do you like being around them?

   b. Structured—Formally interview people, let's call them Informants, who are doing what you might wish to do. To find these Informants, first approach people you know and ask for leads. If they have no suggestions, search the telephone advertising pages, the internet, and magazine or newspaper advertisements. Call them and ask if you may meet or talk to them for fifteen minutes about their career, as you are considering the same. Or you might take them to lunch if they seem receptive. When you meet, politely and respectfully draw them out about the career: how they started, what is a typical day, what they like and do not like about their work, and the lessons they have learned thus far. *Do not ask for a job or a lead.* (Of course, if they offer, feel free to listen.)

If You Are Resisting

If you are postponing, bored by, or resisting gathering initial facts about your Maybe List, consider that the career direction might not be the one for you. For example, when I thought I wanted to go to law school, the fact that I did not bother to talk to one single lawyer or read anything on the topic should have been a clue the size of a law book.

Pay attention to non-action. Is there something on your list that you now see you are not really interested in? Feel free to cross it off. Maybe it is your family's idea of your next move and not yours. Perhaps it is what excites your best friend but not you.

More Facts to Find

After you start researching your Maybe List, there are more questions to answer.

Skills

+ What skills do you need in order to succeed in your new career? For example, if you are buying a yoga studio after being a nurse for ten years, should you gain some business skills in addition to your yoga training? If so, which ones—business planning, how to buy a business, sales, marketing, financial planning, leadership, or something else? It is helpful to make a list and to note after each skill whether the skill is mandatory or simply nice to have.

+ After assessing what skills you need, do some initial research into where you might obtain these skills. Books? Courses? Coaches? By partnering with people who have the skills you lack? Without going crazy, get an approximate idea of the cost. Remember, you are not making decisions now, just gathering facts.

Education/Certificates

✦ What certificates do you absolutely need for entry into your possible field? What does it take to acquire the certificate(s)?

✦ What certificates are not mandatory but might enhance your marketability? Have you talked to successful people who (both) do and do not have this additional certificate? Add these to your list above, but note that they are nice to have.

Money

If necessary, how will you finance your career change? But please be careful as you consider this question. I believe that what you focus on, you become. If you constantly sing the "I don't have enough money" chorus, guess what you won't have enough of? Money. Focusing on what you don't have can quickly squash your dream. Thinking "not enough" can even stop you from exploring what you *could* do.

Once a friend enthusiastically told me about a new personal growth course she had taken and asked me if I wanted to join her for the next session. I heard myself asking her, "How much does it cost?" That was my clue that I was not interested, at least not then. If I had been, I would have asked about the cost at some point—but early in the conversation? No. I wanted a roadblock, and money is a well-constructed one.

Right now, notice what you are thinking about money and your new career. Are you using the thoughts of not enough money as an excuse to stay static and to avoid risk? As an excuse to settle for less than who you can be because change is scary? As an excuse to be unfulfilled in career because doing otherwise is too much work?

There are many ways to finance your career move. I used every single one on the list below:

1. Save money by downsizing your current lifestyle. Set your savings goal and stick with it; put yourself on a financial diet. See Appendix C for resources to help.

2. Invest the money you are saving. Again, see Appendix C for resources.

3. Work a second job. Yes, I know it's tiring and draining, but keep in mind why you are doing it.

4. Find a better paying first job. Don't underestimate your skills; see Appendix C.

5. Negotiate a salary or rate increase in your current job, after figuring out the most strategic way to ask.

6. Take out a business, student, or home equity loan while remembering that the joy of receiving the loan approval is followed by the drudgery of paying it back.

7. Sell jewelry or other items. What about a garage sale?

8. Call in your loans—who owes you money?

9. Borrow seed money from a family member or close friend; see #6 above.

What suggestions do you have to add? As you consider, please notice what you are thinking about the list. Are you saying to yourself, "I can't do this. This won't work because…."

Or are you thinking, "Maybe I could do this. It didn't work before, but now maybe it will. Hmmm."

Time

Time is money's sister; she will need to be considered when making a career change since you will have start-up tasks to accomplish. Like watching your thoughts about money, it is important to notice your thoughts about time. Is "I don't have enough time" your mantra? Could thinking "not enough" reinforce your not ever having enough time?

Like money, there are always ways to find more time. A few ideas follow, with further resources in Appendix C:

1. Prioritize career change activities. Set monthly goals. In the next chapter, we will talk about planning.

2. Drop your time wasters. To identify them, watch how you spend your time as carefully as you count calories on a diet. Write down your time wasters in a notebook that you carry with you everywhere.

3. Plan your day. After writing your "to-do" list, highlight the things you *must* finish. Don't move on to lower-priority items until you complete the highlighted tasks.

4. Lower your quality standards. Not keeping the house as orderly means more time for career change. Not buying the latest fashion means both more money and more time.

5. Be realistic. Double the time you imagine it will take when you start something new, so you won't be disappointed when your learning curve kicks in.

Remind yourself that *you* are worth the time you are spending on you. You are!

Reviewing Your Maybe List

After gathering these basic facts about your potential careers, please review your Maybe List. What on your list now smells like last week's lunch? The purpose of the research is two-fold.

One purpose is straightforward: to find out what you might be getting into. The second purpose is to expose you to your new potential field so that your inner self can browse. You are evaluating without thinking and choosing without deciding. As you delve in and investigate, you are naturally sloughing off what does not feel right.

Your wise part, your inner nature, is helping you every step of the way. And if you are tuning in, you are accessing this help even more.

Hidden Assets

After only two weeks of researching teaching versus corporate training, Tania knew she wanted to be a teacher. She lined up the facts about a teaching certificate and then researched the schools in her area. Unfortunately, the public university was filled for the upcoming year, but she found a private school that had room in its program and even fast-tracked the certificate process.

When she saw the price tag, she knew why the school had space. She had stashed away a bit of money but was short—way short.

After twisting her brain in a braid, Tania decided on two things: to get a part-time job and to approach her sister for a loan. The job happened first; she began clerking, for near minimum wage, at a convenience store. The job was far from ideal, but she figured some money was better than none.

Unlike job hunting, talking to her sister went better than Tania expected. Instead of a loan, she received a gift of one semester of tuition.

"Let's see how it goes after a semester," the sister said. "Then we can figure out the rest. But don't worry. I'll help you out. You'll get through school."

Tania then realized one of her hidden assets—people who believed in her.

Chapter 9 Exercises

Research and Tell

1. Begin gathering facts using the questions presented in this chapter for the careers on your Maybe List.

2. Write in a journal or tell a friend the results of your research. What did you find out that surprised you? What do you get excited about? What discouraged you?

3. Continue noticing your thoughts about money and time. What are they? How might they impact you?

Revise Your List

1. How many options do you now have on your Maybe List?

2. Review your list. Touch each choice with your finger. How do you feel? Are you excited? Nervous? Bored? Scared? Assign at least one emotion for each option you have.

3. Cross off an item from your list if it feels flat and out of date to you. Was that difficult or easy to do?

Chapter 9 Summary

Good work! In this chapter, you worked from the logical, left side of your brain to investigate the options you discovered. By researching your options, you also began the weeding process and may have removed some options from your Maybe List. Digging into the facts—through research and by talking to others already in the field—will make your dream more real.

***

Next, join me as I meet the woman who helped me to discover *nine* pivotal words that helped me on my new career journey.

10:
Discover Your Guiding Star

When I answered the Aunt Clara question, I said I would write and speak and that my audience would be women. But I had no other clues. What exactly would I write about? Talk about? My passion hid from me, so I began attending evening seminars by female writers and speakers to hear what they had to say and to hear the questions women in the audience asked. I didn't know it, but I was also looking for something else.

All of the speakers were excellent. Then I attended an evening with Shakti Gawain, author of the best-selling book, *Creative Visualization*. About five hundred New Yorkers filled a Midtown hotel ballroom that night. When Ms. Gawain walked onto the stage and began speaking, I literally gasped. My inner self recognized the role model I needed.

Ms. Gawain was not a rah-rah motivational speaker, but she was engaging. Foremost, she was sincere. She exuded lived-in knowledge about her topic and combined it with the courage and passion to share it, in an intelligent and compelling way, to a ballroom full of people.

And then there was her topic. Creative visualization was metaphysical but practical. It was right-brain material and was presented in a left-brain way. Ms. Gawain spoke each audience member's whole being. She was holistic.

When I saw and heard her, my inner coach said softly but with conviction nine key words, "If she can do it, I can do it." She was my Guiding Star.

Who is the Next You?

Many women inspire me: Eleanor Roosevelt, Jacqueline Kennedy Onassis, Mother Theresa, Princess Diana, and Oprah Winfrey. But they are icons.

What I would like you to do is to find the woman who is doing what you wish you were doing and to whom you can relate. She might be many steps ahead of you on the journey, or only a few. She might be someone you know, or a stranger. She might be famous or not. But when you see her, your inner self will resonate with recognition of the qualities that you, one day, will display. You will feel and say, appreciatively, "If she can do it, I can do it."

When you say that, you won't just resonate with her outward appearance, words, or actions. Your inner being will sense her inner qualities and acknowledge similarities with your own. You will map out who you can become on the inside, which will lead to what you will manifest on the outside. It's an instinctual, right-brain activity, and it begins with a flash or feeling of recognition.

Stick with your Gender

If you are a female reader, I recommend that you limit your search for a guiding star to other women. This is important because women and men think, speak, and act differently from each other (as is well-covered in *Men are from Mars, Women are from Venus* by John Gray). Girls and boys have different experiences growing up and different obstacles once grown. While we all experience the human condition, that condition is different across gender lines.

When we try to map what we as women want to do with what a man is doing, we meet subtle *internal* confusion. Our deeper selves know our inner qualities will not manifest in the same manner as they manifest on the object of our mapping, so we cannot quite get behind the task.

This is not to say that you cannot learn from men. You may have, as I have, learned oodles from wonderful male teachers and mentors. But if you wish to be galvanized into certainty and action, search for your Guiding Star within your gender. She is there.

The Inner Search

Since your inner self is the one who becomes confused when you model yourself upon a man, turn to her for help in finding your Guiding Star. First, before you go to sleep, instruct your deeper self to help you find the woman about whom you can inwardly say, "If she can do it, I can do it." You can instruct her silently, out loud, or by writing the instruction.

You are asking for help during sleep because that is when the conscious, thinking mind is least active to block the instruction. When you sleep, you won't voice objections like, "That doesn't make sense," or "What? Are you crazy? That will never work!"

Instead, your inner nature is free to do her magic. You may have dreams or visions. You may wake up in the morning knowing what to do. Or you may feel nothing upon waking, only to find yourself drawn to just the right class or encountering just the right friend of a friend.

The Outer Search

After asking for help, take action. From the glimpses you received from the Aunt Clara exercise, look for the woman who inspires and empowers you through:

1. The Informants you'll meet when gathering facts (see chapter 9)

2. Friends or family (However, if you hesitate to ask a particular friend or family member, say nothing. Your intuition is asking you to hold off on revealing your budding dream.)

3. The Internet

4. Adult education courses such as those offered through the Learning Annex

5. The company where you work

6. Networking and professional groups

7. Training courses

8. Books and magazines

The good part is you don't even have to know what you're looking for. Your intuition will pop ideas out; and if you're open, you'll grab them. You will find yourself meeting your Guiding Star at just the right moment. Also, it's important to note that she might not do exactly what you end up doing, but she might have the *lifestyle* you want to model.

Be sure to relax. This isn't a talent search or research for a term paper. It's fun and unstressful. Your soul is doing the searching; you just need to be awake.

In Person is Important

Since energy is transmitted between people best in person, you may not find your Guiding Star until you see her in person. Once you see her, you may or may not take any further steps. I never spoke to or emailed Shakti Gawain, though this chapter is a belated thank you to her. On the other hand, the woman who was my Guiding Star in project management, Paula Martin, became both a mentor and a friend.

What will you do? Listen to yourself and see.

Chapter 10 Exercises

Guiding Star

1. Practice the inner search for your Guiding Star, as outlined in this chapter. Do this every evening for at least three days.

2. Now begin your outer search, but slowly. Keep your eyes and ears open.

3. Relax and have fun; you will find her. In the meantime, you can continue with other exercises. The universe has its own timing.

Chapter 10 Summary

Excellent! You are on a gentle search for the woman who will inspire you to say, "If she can do it, I can do it." She will help you realize that your career dream is not impossible; she is living, breathing proof of its possibility. Your inner self will help you to find her at exactly the right time for you.

***

In the next chapter, we will look at a dream stopper—fear. Can you imagine turning down a job in paradise? That's what I did.

11:
Noticing

When I was in graduate school, I interned with the Service Employees International Union thinking that I might be suited to union organizing. At the same time, I took an evening class in labor negotiations offered by the local community college. When I graduated, the SEIU local waved me goodbye but the negotiating instructor, also from a union, said his union had an opening for an organizer in Hawaii. Was I interested?

Was I? I needed a job. I wanted to be an organizer. And Hawaii? Living on the islands should have been as enticing as a swim in a warm ocean at night.

Instead, I felt, deep in my stomach, afraid. "You can't do this," a voice screamed inside my head. "You can't do this." Even though the job was what I wanted, working so far away was scarier than a hundred horror movies.

Now, when presented with a career opportunity that scares me, I have learned to sleep on the possibility. But my twenty-eight-year-old self only knew fear, and flatly said no. I probably was not breathing.

I know there are millions of women who face the unknown like trapeze artists swing, high above us, from rope to rope. I am not one of them.

The Disguises of Fear

Many things worth doing in life feel, at first, like fear supreme served on a platter—that I learned from babysitting. Since we're talking about career change, I couldn't sleep at night if we didn't talk about fear and how to minimize it.

> Babysitting Lesson #1: It's normal to be scared when starting a new career.

Fear is the biggest block we face. But fear is tricky. It will show up in other disguises like:

✦ Procrastination

✦ Confusion

✦ Uncertainty

✦ Judging yourself and others

✦ Impatience

✦ A "Why bother?" attitude

✦ Playing the victim

✦ "I'm not worth it anyway" feeling

✦ Negativity of all sorts and persuasions

And sometimes fear is bold-faced, as it was for me when I was offered the job in Hawaii.

Maybe I was right to turn down that job. Maybe I was not ready to jump away from my support system then. For it is not the decision that I regret, but the takeover. When we are in fear's grip, we don't choose; fear decides and speaks for us, and it mostly says no.

Would you like to know a gentle way out?

One Antidote to Fear

Buddhists have a practice called "mindfulness." It is a method of watching yourself from an observer's vantage point. Let's say you are talking on the telephone. If you were practicing mindfulness, most of your attention would be engaged in the conversation. But another tiny sliver would be watching you as you talk. This sliver would notice when you disengage from the conversation and wonder what's for dinner. Notice when you wish the conversation were over but keep talking for politeness' sake. Notice when enough is enough and you guide the conversation to a close.

This sliver is the inner self. Mindfulness is a practice of engaging the inner self in our everyday, ordinary life—and not just when we are tuning in. This is important because your inner self has the power to speed transformation and change and to whittle fear down to size.

Not Judging is the Hard Part

Mindfulness is the practice of noticing, but with one catch: noticing is done without judging. ("Sure, right," you might be thinking. "Without judging? Without criticizing?") In the above example, you would have no judgment that your mind wandered during the telephone conversation; no judgment that you did not bring the conversation to a close sooner; and no judgment that you ended the conversation when you did, even if the other person wanted to talk more.

We are all challenged to observe without judging, since our childhood judges now live inside of us (which could be why it feels so crowded at times). But the challenge is as rewarding as a luxurious vacation at your dream destination. By noticing—simply noticing—we come to accept who we are, warts and all. And with this acceptance, self-sabotaging behavior quietly falls away.

And what do you do if you keep judging and don't get to the simply watching phase? Easy. You notice that you are judging. As you notice, it too will pass.

Mindfulness—like most things that seem initially difficult—becomes easier over time, as Allison saw.

Good-Girl Praise

While tuning in helped Allison to turn down the hate knob on her job, she wanted more than that. "I think I'll need to go back to school for whatever career option shakes out," she told me. "And the money I'm earning on this job will really help me to save. Is there something else that can help me now besides tuning in?"

I told her how to practice mindfulness. "Just watch your thoughts," I said. "Observe yourself."

"That's all?" she said.

"It sounds simple," I replied. "But start slowly. It helps in the beginning to just focus on one task. Begin tonight, when you brush your teeth. Focus on nothing else but brushing your teeth. Be aware both of what you are doing and what you are thinking. By only doing one simple task, it will make it easier to watch your thoughts."

As predicted, Allison had a harder time staying focused than she thought she would. But she kept setting aside "focus times" and gradually improved. Soon, she took her skill to work.

As you may recall, Allison's number one complaint at work was her boss who criticized her and then criticized her some more. So I asked Allison to observe herself around her boss. What did she think? How did she act? How did she feel?

After two weeks of noticing, Allison reported that she felt like a little girl in need of approval from her boss. She had no idea who her boss stood for in her psyche—if anyone—for she was nothing like Allison's mother or any authority figure she could remember. But Allison began to see how she felt bad when her boss did not comment on her work and worse when she nitpicked. "It's not like I want to get ahead at that company. All I want to do is leave. But still I feel bad when I don't get the approval I think I deserve, when I'm not recognized for how…"

"Good you are?" I interrupted.

"Yes. How did you know?"

Easy. I had recognized part of myself in Allison. Those of us who received praise as girls for being good—following the rules, being dependable and responsible, neat and courteous— have receptors in our neural pathways for good-girl praise. We grow afraid when we do not receive it. As adults, we still harvest those pathways for external praise. Only slowly do we learn that the trail to follow is within.

I told Allison how long it had taken me to realize that being addicted to someone else's approval stemmed from fear. "Every woman isn't like you and me. Some women I know are fearless. But for me, fear is in my DNA. I can't completely eliminate it but neither can I let it stop me."

Allison listened. "So what do I do?" she asked. "I want to follow my boss's directions and meet her standards. But I don't want to feel afraid."

"All I can tell you," I said, "is more of the same. Notice. Notice without judging when you want to be noticed or when you want approval. It will take time, but gradually your addiction for approval will decrease. By observing, you are inviting your deeper self into your life, and it is your deeper self who can replace your need for approval with acceptance and joy for who you really are, underneath the addiction."

Undoing the Good-Girl Stuff

When we spoke again in two weeks, Allison said the image of being a good girl stuck in her head. She took it a step further. When she noticed that she ached for approval, she pictured herself in a dress with a crisply starched apron and a huge bow in her hair—the embodiment of a Victorian-era very, very good girl.

By exaggerating her thoughts and feelings, she more clearly noticed them—and watched as they decreased. She said it was like watching ice turn into water. You can't pinpoint the moment that it happens, but it does.

"Will you tell me again why noticing works?" she asked. "Why do my thoughts change just because I become aware of them?"

I answered, "Acceptance. You aren't resisting your thoughts any longer. You are accepting them, and so they don't have to fight to stay alive. They can leave your mind. Your inner self can shake them off like a dust mop shedding dirt."

Within a month, Allison had learned not to let her boss's criticism affect her so much; most of the time she shrugged it off. She still had to clean up her relationship with her co-workers, another source of frustration at work. She had already dealt with fear #1, so how hard could it be?

Keep it Simple

If you have experienced major childhood trauma, noticing might only be a partial answer. First, you may need to enlist professional therapeutic help. But if noticing does feel like the right start, it's easy to begin. Start with noticing your thoughts, since they are the source of your feelings and actions. The focus you gain from tuning in will help you to be mindful.

If you want to keep a journal of your noticing, feel free. But it is not necessary. Keep it simple. Just notice.

Chapter 11 Exercises

Noticing

1. Pick something you are slightly afraid of doing or intimidated by. If you cannot think of anything, select a task that comes into your mind when you think "procrastination."

2. Decide when, within the next three days, you will do this.

3. As you are doing it, notice your thoughts and feelings. Where in your body do you feel bodily sensations? Could these be fear?

4. For taking action despite your fear, reward yourself in any way you would like. Though treating myself is not one of my strong points, here are some examples: take a bubble bath, call a friend, sneak in a hike, or eat that treat you don't normally allow yourself.

5. Write in a journal or tell a friend of your experience.

Chapter 11 Summary

You are courageous! Talking about fear is never a light subject, but necessary, since it is the biggest dream blocker. We talked about fear and its disguises, and also about a method of melting fear. That method is mindfulness, which is noticing thoughts, feelings, and actions without judgment. It is the second inner key of the stress-free way. Mindfulness develops the same mental muscles as the first inner key, tuning in. Noticing also engages your inner self in your everyday, ordinary life—including your new career journey.

***

Every journey requires some planning. Career changes are no exception, so we will rejoin Carmen as she plans for her next business and creative venture.

12:
Planning

Carmen was ecstatic! She found a business partner to handle the business side of her jewelry business, unburdening her from the work she didn't like. It also gave her time to research her possible next moves.

During research, she dropped the idea of illustrating children's books. But the more she investigated storytelling, the more enthused she became. In fact, she was making herself crazy with all that she had to learn and do.

"Why don't you put together a plan?" I suggested.

"A plan? I don't want to make a project out of this," she told me. "A plan would take out all the fun. I might feel pressured to do certain things by certain times."

"But you're feeling overwhelmed thinking of all you have to do, right?" I persisted.

"Yeah…"

"So put a high-level plan on your wall using adhesive notes. You can always change the sticky notes around as things change."

She was not convinced, but neither did she protest. It was a start.

Planning Simplified

Planning is important because you let loose—on paper—the plans and actions that are buzzing in your head like hornets. My project management friends are now shrinking in pain that I am not saying more about the benefits of planning, for there is more to say. But let's keep it simple while noting that:

✦ The value of a plan primarily comes from the process of planning

✦ Plans are made to be revised; an unrevised plan is an unused one

✦ Planning is a tool you can use at any point of a career move—even during the Discovery phase when your right-brain creative neurons fire most brightly

Begin with a Goal

Like knowing where you will end up on a trip, start your planning with a goal. In the Zooming In phase, your goal might be "to gather facts about my career possibilities" or "to validate the career ideas on my Maybe List." In the space below, please write your Zooming In goal. It could be the same as the examples I just gave.

Goal:_____

_____

Since Carmen now had only one idea on her Maybe List, her goal was "to find out whether storytelling is a viable career."

Difference between an Activity and a Milestone

In the beginning, keep your planning at the milestone, not activity, level. What's a milestone? What's an activity? Pretend you are driving across the United States, or another spread-out country. Because it is holiday season, you need to make hotel or motel reservations for each night or risk sleeping in the car. With a map, it is easy. You:

✦ Decide upon the route

✦ Decide how long you want to drive each day

✦ Pick your nightly stopping points, using the map's calculation of the mileage between cities

The nightly stops are the *milestones* of your trip.

To reach the milestones, you perform *activities*. You wake up, drive the car, put fuel in the car, stop for meals, buy water, and play music. Activities are tasks performed to reach a milestone.

Carmen's Zooming In milestones were to:

1. Complete book research

2. Finish Internet research of storytelling websites

3. Finish research of storytelling associations

4. Complete research of storytelling conferences

5. Complete research of storytelling courses

6. Talk to at least three storytellers

7. Make list of what she needed to do to become a storyteller

Carmen decided she wanted to finish these milestones in two months.

The Sticky-Note Method

You know sticky notes, right? They have adhesive at the top of one side and come in different sizes and colors? I asked Carmen to:

1. Buy sticky notes in at least two different colors—the brighter the better but not the smallest size.

2. Using all one color, write her career change milestones on the sticky notes, one milestone per sticky note.

3. Using the other color, write the name of the month she would begin on one sticky note. Then, with the same color, write the next month on the next note.

4. Put the first month on the wall and vertically underneath it place the milestones she would complete that month.

5. Do the same for the second month. When finished, her wall looked like Figure 12-1, the Sticky Notes diagram.

The sticky-note method worked fine for Carmen, who, despite her resistance to planning, was organized and disciplined. Every day, she looked at the month's milestones on her wall. Looking at the milestones reminded her where she was and where she was going. Then, when she wrote her "to-do" list for the day, she included activities that led to the milestones.

Carmen said that she liked having the milestones on her wall, in a form that could be moved around as needed, because it didn't make her feel like a bureaucrat crafting a five-year plan.

The Sticky-Note Method
Figure 12-1

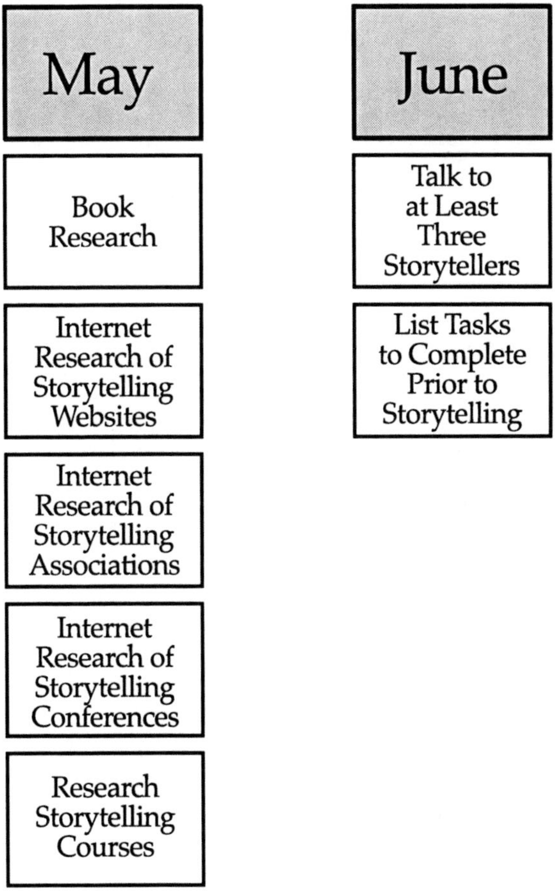

May	June
Book Research	Talk to at Least Three Storytellers
Internet Research of Storytelling Websites	List Tasks to Complete Prior to Storytelling
Internet Research of Storytelling Associations	
Internet Research of Storytelling Conferences	
Research Storytelling Courses	

While milestone planning worked for Carmen, you might want more details if you are more detailed oriented or simply would like more structure.

If Carmen had created such a plan, either on a spreadsheet in her computer or on a sheet of paper by hand, it might look like Table 12-1.

TABLE 12-1:

MILESTONES	ACTIVITIES	FINISH BY
Book Research	Go to bookstores	5/3
	Search for books online	5/5
	Read books	5/31
Internet Research of Storytelling Websites	Search Google	5/6
	Search Yahoo	5/6
	Decide what other search engines to search	5/12
	Other searches	5/12
Internet Research of Storytelling Associations	Same search engines as above; may come across when doing research above	5/31
Internet Research of Storytelling Conferences	Same search engines as above; may come across when doing research above	5/31
Research Storytelling Courses	Same search engines as above; may come across when doing research above	5/31

Talk to at Least Three Storytellers	Make list of who to contact	6/5
	Call or email to request conversation	6/8
	Make list of questions	6/8
	Have conversations	6/28
	Follow-up thank you	6/29
List of Tasks to Complete Prior to Storytelling	Finish draft	6/30

The expanded plan takes longer to create and to revise, but gives more detail and provides time frames within the month. And, even if you use the detailed plan, you can still have the milestones on sticky notes on your wall.

Chapter 12 Exercises

Planning

1. Decide which type of plan you would like to use for exercise: sticky note alone or sticky note plus the more detailed one.

2. Choose a phase you will plan for: Discovery or Zooming In.

3. Create a plan. If you choose Discovery, you can use the checklist at the end of chapter 8 for milestone ideas.

4. Ask a friend who knows you well to review your plan and to give you feedback. Are you being too ambitious? Expecting to change the world in a week?

5. Revise your plan—and keep revising as you go along.

Checklist of the Zooming In Phase

Once again, we are ending a phase. If you like checklists, feel free to complete the one below. If not, move on to the Summary.

❏ I have read books about the fields on my Maybe List.

❏ I have completed internet research.

❏ I have completed _____ (fill in the number) Informant interviews.

❏ I have found my Guiding Star (role model).

❏ I know what skills I must acquire.

❏ I have completed initial research on how to acquire the skills.

❏ I know what education or certificates I must have, and how to obtain them.

❏ I know what education or certificates are optional.

❏ I know approximately how much money my career move will cost.

❏ I have investigated _____ (fill in the number) ways to raise money.

❏ I am becoming more aware of my thoughts and how they impact me.

❏ I have completed a sticky note plan for my move, or one more detailed strategy.

Zooming In Activities

See Figure 12-2 for Zooming In Activities

Zooming in Phase Activities
Figure 12-2

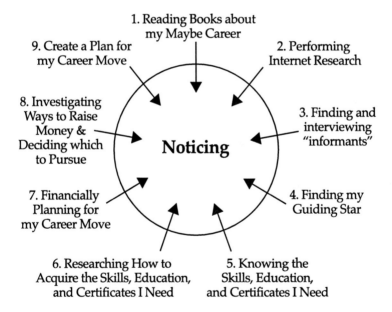

Chapter 12 Summary

Celebrate! You've finished planning and the Zooming In phase. For planning, you reviewed the sticky-note method as well as a more detailed approach. You know that plans are made to be broken, and the value of a plan is in the planning. In the next chapter, have fun trying on.

PART 3
Moving On

13:
Trying On

I met Jill at a conference. When she found out about this book, she told me her story.

Jill was a software developer who had worked for the same large corporation for twenty years. Longing for a change, she decided to start her own software consulting company. Jill dove into researching and then planning. She developed a beautiful project plan and executed it perfectly. She incorporated her company, built a website, rented an office, ordered business cards, and designed a brochure. Finally, she quit her job.

Then she waited. And waited. Unfortunately, she had no clients.

Six months later and $75,000 poorer, Jill returned to her old company.

Online Shopping and Career

I love online shopping but I would never buy an expensive dress, one that I had not tried on before, from an internet shop.

Moving to a new career without trying it on first is a thousand times worse than buying a closet full of non-returnable, internet-purchased dresses—a risky investment!

It is easy to see that Jill should have skipped the "fluff"—the cards, brochure, office, and website—and focused on the clients. She could have worked part-time while still maintaining her full-time job, then quit when she knew she had clients for her services.

Jill told me the lesson she learned was invaluable, though painful. She said she had not given up on starting her own business, but next time would start in small steps before quitting her paying job and would make sure people wanted what she had to sell.

Oh, how I want you to avoid Jill's mistake! You can try on your new career in a variety of ways while you stick with your current job.

- ✦ **Volunteering**—Many non-profit and cultural organizations have active volunteer programs. But you can even volunteer your time at a business by explaining that you'll trade your time for the experience. While a huge corporation will probably not agree, smaller-size businesses may be more open.

- ✦ **Interning**—Often colleges and trade schools offer internships as part of a course of study. When you research schools, be sure to ask about the internship opportunities, or create one yourself.

- ✦ **Provide Services for Free**—This is the route that I took to try out the stress-free methodology. By developing your services and offering them for free in the beginning, you can try on, receive feedback, and improve. At the same time, you will gain clients who are happy to refer you to their friends when you do begin charging.

✦ **Courses**—Sometimes all it takes to persuade or dissuade you is an ounce of exposure, the type you receive through class discussion and assignments. Evening classes at community colleges are a low-cost way to begin trying on your new career.

If it seems daunting to start your new career while continuing the old, take note that even Albert Einstein, when beginning his scientific career, worked as a patents clerk during the day and wrote physics papers at night. (Granted, he probably did not clean house or care for the kids.)

Time Off

When I shifted from my consulting career to my present one, I tried it on by writing, speaking, and mentoring for free. But there was a point when I intuitively knew I had to quit the day job in order to make room for the new passion—even before the passion paid the bills. Since I had downsized, saved, and invested, I financed the lag time myself, after carefully listening to my intuition on the timing.

Be careful with this alternative. It is attractive, since we all need sabbaticals. But it can be costly in terms of time, money, and self-esteem if the timing is not correct. Your intuition, which we cover in the next chapter, will help you know if and when taking time off is right for you.

Notice If You Stop Trying On

If we don't bother to try on our new career possibility—as I didn't when I thought I wanted to be a lawyer—it could be that the career is not the one. Or maybe it is, but now is not the right time. Trying on will give you answers, whether you want them or not.

If you are not trying on your new possible career, pay attention. Why aren't you? What would it hurt to try on? What could you gain?

> Babysitting Lesson #6: Career can take you out of your comfort zone—and that's a good thing!

Second Guessing

When Tania was deciding whether to be a corporate trainer or a teacher, she spoke with friends who were both. She also volunteered in her daughter's classroom and observed a teacher friend at work. Though she knew the business world better, she chose teaching as her new career.

A year-and-a-half later, with her teacher's certificate and many hours of in-class experience, Tania questioned her decision—because she could not find a job. "Did I eliminate training too soon?" she asked me. "Did I make the right decision?"

Since it's easy to see how second-guessing drains energy when someone else does it, I told her that replaying the teaching-or-training decision only limited her ability to be in the present. Second-guessing drained her energy. In addition, I reminded her that impatience masks fear. Like children, we want life to happen on our time schedule.

"And I should just notice when I second-guess or am impatient, right?" she asked, sighing.

"Right." I answered. I like it when people catch on, even if they question the value.

Soon after, Tania heard about a temporary position as a corporate trainer. She applied, and found herself a customer service trainer the next week. She was thrilled, and not just because of the much needed paycheck. She had already experienced teaching. Now life gave her the opportunity to try on training.

Within a month, Tania unequivocally knew what her new career would be—teaching. Training reminded her of what she did not like about the corporate environment. It also reinforced how much she wanted to be around young minds, whether or not they were eager for her instruction.

Tania's certainty reignited her job search. In late August, she received a call from a high school that unexpectedly needed a teacher, and convinced them she was the one they wanted.

Chapter 13 Exercises

Trying On

1. What are you doing or what will you do to try on your new career? What might you add from the list in this chapter?

2. If you wish to add additional try-on steps, when will you start and finish them?

3. If you are not planning to try-on your new career, write in your journal or tell a friend why not. What do you notice when you write or talk?

Chapter 13 Summary

Congratulations! You have completed yet another crucial step in your new career journey. By trying on a career before committing to it, you will save yourself time and expense, headache and heartache. By taking action, you put yourself in the real world to validate or refine your vision. While the ways to try on are as unlimited as your imagination, they include volunteering your time, internships, offering your services for free, and hands-on courses.

Throughout your career change, listening to your intuition can create jumpstarts and shortcuts.

$$***$$

In the next chapter, we will rejoin Rachel as she saves time and energy by following her instincts.

14:
Just Knowing

Rachel, who surprised herself by liking the practice of tuning in, startled herself even further by waking up twenty minutes earlier to meditate in the mornings. She did it because she enjoyed starting her day with more energy and clarity.

After two months of quieting her thoughts—combined with noticing them throughout the day—Rachel grew concerned.

"I'm not my usual self," she said. "Sometimes I know what to do without even thinking about it. It's so weird."

"Like what?" I asked.

"Well, the other day I was trying to figure out whether I should take a real estate class or not. I had never heard of the training company before, but it sounded like it would be worthwhile. Instead of agonizing about the decision, I just knew I should take the course. It was a feeling inside of me, a gut feeling."

"That's not so weird," I told her. "You had an intuition, a hunch. You're operating at a faster speed. Thinking is slow compared to receiving information from your inner self."

"But how can I trust it?" she said. "What if the course turns out to be awful?"

So I taught Rachel three ways to validate and increase the information she received outside of her five senses: checking in with common sense, figuring out her intuitive mode, and starting small.

Check in with Common Sense

"Intuition doesn't have to violate common sense," I told Rachel. "While there might be some intuitions that make no sense at all, they are few and far between. Most of the time, intuition and common sense go hand-in-hand."

When I asked her whether it made sense to attend the class, Rachel said she had a policy never to take a course that had not been personally recommended to her.

I asked if she could ask the company for referrals.

"I suppose," she said.

As we talked further, Rachel admitted that she didn't like things to interrupt her plans; she had planned for a course from another source and finding this one upset her plans.

"Ah, all the more reason to follow the hunch!" I said.

Your Intuitive Mode

Rachel's intuition came in the form of a strong bodily feeling; she called it a gut instinct. Other people receive intuitive information in other ways, such as:

✦ feeling that you just know something, and always have

✦ image or other visual clue

✦ feeling of lightness and buoyancy

✦ feeling of rightness or certainty

✦ reaction or response in your body

By becoming aware of the way she received information, I told Rachel she could learn to recognize—and trust—the nudge more and more. While her instincts would not always speak to her in the same way, in the beginning, at least, relying on her dominant mode would help her to listen and trust.

Start Small

I encouraged Rachel to listen to her intuition in relatively unimportant matters in the beginning. She could intuit the right outfit to wear or the best route to take to work. After her intuitive sense became accustomed to being asked for advice and of being followed, the volume would increase.

Rachel did this, and then we talked.

"So, what is your intuition telling you about the course now?" I asked.

"To take it," she answered.

"Does your intuition align with common sense?"

"Yes," she answered. "I've done my homework about the course. People who took the course before really liked it." She paused. "You know, I feel more trusting now. I will take the class."

So she did.

When I saw her later she said the course was excellent, but what she learned about herself was better: she learned that she did *not* want to pursue real estate after all. "Maybe my intuition was being so insistent," she mused, "so that it could save me the time and money of going down the wrong path. It pushed me to find the best course to try on real estate so that I could see it's not for me."

Intuition and Planning

Let's rescue Carmen from her sticky notes by checking in with her. As she progressed in quieting her mind through sketching every morning, which was her alternative to tuning in, she also experienced an upswing in intuition. Carmen then used her instincts to refine her day.

Since Carmen was very visual, often a picture flashed in her mind of what she should put at the top of her "to-do" list. Other days she would see an image of a jewelry design or pass by a store she just knew she should approach about selling her jewelry. As she found herself getting more done than she ever imagined she could, she learned to welcome and trust her insights more.

Why Intuition Works

Recall that intuitions reside below our conscious mind—in the larger part of the iceberg. They are nudges from our subconscious that bubble up constantly. Perhaps you have:

+ known the phone was going to ring before it did

+ answered a friend's question before she even asked it

+ sat next to a stranger at a conference who introduced you to someone you'd been trying to meet for years

+ on a whim bought something that you unexpectedly needed the next day

◆ met someone whom you immediately felt could
be a long-term friend—and they became one

These are all examples of our intuition leading our slower part, the clunky, top-of-the-iceberg mind, through life. (I call this part of the mind clunky because it is often trapped in the past, bothered with worries, chattering about nonsense, or stuck in fear.)

Intuitions arise because we are more than our conscious mind. They work because we are human beings and not machines; however, the more "logically" robotic we are, the less intuition is available.

The less we listen to our intuition, the harder it is to hear it.

Intuition and Tuning In

Rachel and Carmen experienced upswings in their intuition when they began quieting their minds. Noisy minds block intuitive messages. It's hard for a gut feeling to be felt if you live in your head and rarely notice how your body feels. It's hard for an image to appear if your mind is in knots. Quieting and unknotting the mind and paying attention to the body give intuition much-needed cultivation— or rather, re-cultivation—space.

We were all probably more intuitive as children than we are today. Education heavily relies on left-brain logical thinking. When we are adults, we then assume that problems can be "figured out." Not true. You've probably heard the quote by the career-changing Albert Einstein, "We can't solve problems by using the same kind of thinking we used when we created them."

When I was a child, I was naturally intuitive. Now I am finding my way back to that natural just-knowing state. Whether I've fully returned yet or not, I don't know. I certainly had not when the following took place.

Intuition Ignored

One morning, when I was living and working in Manhattan, I finished dressing for work and went to the closet to pick out a pair of shoes to wear to work. I had the intuition to wear a thick-soled, very comfortable sandal that day. But my inner *fashionista* reasoned that I had worn those shoes the day before, and should not start an ugly-but-comfortable trend. Ignoring the intuition, even when it grew stronger, I strapped on a pair of thin-soled, slightly uncomfortable, dressy sandals. "After all," I reasoned, "I only have to walk to the taxi outside the apartment. It's not like I'm walking the three blocks to the subway." Outside of my apartment, I easily found a taxi to Midtown.

The day was uneventful until mid-afternoon when my computer shut off, along with the office overhead lights. At the time, I was talking to a friend in lower Manhattan, who said her lights were off, too. Fearing the worst, I looked out the window and saw thousands of people pouring out of surrounding office buildings, crowding the sidewalks and street.

It was August 14, 2003, the day of the Northeast U.S. electrical shutdown. New York City, at first nervously and then jubilantly, skidded to a halt.

I walked home six miles to Tribeca, the neighborhood where I lived. My shoes went from slightly uncomfortable to extremely uncomfortable. Blisters grew. The soles felt thinner with every concrete block. I tried not to think about my comfortable walking shoes in my closet, and the intuition I had to wear them that day.

Chapter 14 Exercises

Beginning Intuition

1. What is your mode of receiving intuitive information? If you do not know, you can easily find out by noticing.

2. The best practice you can do for increasing your intuition is the tuning in exercise of chapter 6. If you have not started tuning in, consider beginning now.

Intuition and Career

1. How would you rate your ability to listen to your intuition on a scale of 1 to 4, with 4 being the highest?

2. If you would like to increase your intuition, start small. Check in with your intuition every day to sense:

   ✦ What should you wear to work?

   ✦ When should you stop in to see the boss?

   ✦ When is the best time to go to lunch?

   ✦ What work activities should you push and which need time to take root?

   Where possible, validate your choice. For example, if you chose to wear a particular scarf one day, what happened as a result? Did a client comment on it, setting off a conversation? Did simply wearing the scarf give you just the boost you needed that day? In the beginning, draw a link between your intuition and the effects, even though some of the effects will not be consciously known.

3.   Write in your journal or tell a friend about your experiments in listening to your intuition, as we all tend to discount these discoveries. What is the most challenging? The most rewarding?

Chapter 14 Summary

Pat yourself on the back! You have reached the third and final inner key, just knowing. Just knowing follows tuning in and noticing as the basis of the stress-free way. When you listen to your intuition in your career move, you can move faster and further than you imagined possible.

Intuition is available twenty-four hours a day and increases as we quiet our minds through tuning in. As we develop our intuitive abilities, we can validate our hunches through common sense, figuring out our intuitive mode, and by starting small. And we can always increase our abilities.

***

In the next chapter, we will visit commitment. Commitment is not as final-final as it sounds. I'll show you how I did it step-by-step.

15:
Committing,
Step-by-Step

Before I committed to my most recent career change, I dabbled with leaving project management "someday." While different careers crossed my mind, the one that stuck was screenwriting. Someday, I would become a screenwriter.

I had fallen in love with movies when I was ten years old. As a reward for being a volunteer librarian (as if I needed one), I received a Saturday afternoon pass to the State Theater. It was the only movie theater in town, and a Saturday pass meant a double feature—all summer long!

For some reason, my usually vigilant mother paid no attention to what was playing when she dropped me off and picked me up four hours later. As a result, I learned about adult life from movies like *Peyton Place* and *Rome Adventure*: romance, glamour, babies out of wedlock, affairs. From Westerns, war movies, and my all-time-favorite, *Gone with the Wind*, I viewed heroism and courage. Movies opened my eyes to a broader world.

Years later, it was no wonder that screenwriting became my "someday" career. I dreamed about the screenplay I would write someday, dreamed about being the oldest-ever screenwriter to receive an Academy Award, and, naturally, imagined what I would wear when I accepted my Oscar.

Finally, I decided to do something. First, I read a how-to book on screenwriting. Then, I took a course at The New School taught by someone who enjoyed reminiscing about his Hollywood days. Though we didn't make it to a screen treatment, the course was fun and gave me a path to follow to learn this craft.

Three months later, I noticed that I had written absolutely nothing.

Then I met Richard. Richard had written and directed a movie that I had never heard of, but that he said could be rented at any video store. He now wanted to be a project manager; I coached him in project management and he coached me in screenwriting.

First, he showed me what a screenplay actually looked like. Yuck! What were those camera shot directions doing in the script? Wasn't that the director's job to figure that out?

Second, he showed me what a discouraged screenwriter looked like and sounded like. Richard had turned to project management because he was getting nowhere with his second screenplay; even his agent no longer returned his calls.

"Marina," he told me, "don't get into this business unless you really have to."

If I had been committed to screenwriting, I would have heard his words and pressed on.

Instead, I put my screenwriting books away. Though I still love movies, I'm happy to let someone else be the oldest screenwriter to win an Oscar.

Step-by-Step Commitment

According to the Oxford Dictionary, to commit means "to pledge, involve, or bind, especially oneself." A commitment is an inner decision reflected in the outer world.

Like everything else we have covered, committing to a new career works best step by step. Committing to screenwriting pushed me out of the dreaming phase. And decommitting allowed me to find my true passion—conversing with you about career and spirit.

Easy Way to Know if You're Committed

It is easy to know what you have pledged yourself to: it is what you are doing now. What are your commitments? Just look at what you are doing now. How do you spend your time? Who do you spend time with? These activities and people are your commitments.

Sometimes we say we are committed to change, but we are not acting on our commitment because we have no time or money, or because another person comes first. I have two comments on that.

First, read Cynthia Kersey's book *Unstoppable Women* for example after example of women who did commit—and accomplished—despite a dizzying array of obstacles.

Second, remember that we can de-commit. Sometimes other people must be consulted before we formally de-commit. But most of our broken commitments are to ourselves. And what do you think of a person who commits and does not follow through? Whatever it is, that is what you think of yourself when your commitment gets lower priority than dirty laundry.

Because I spent so long in the dreaming phase, I urge you to learn from my mistakes. You're almost at the end of this book. Commit to something. Re-read the book, but this time, do the exercises. Go to The Pink Edge website www.pinkedge.com and browse the "free stuff" section.

Take a questionnaire. Do whatever your intuition directs. But do something as a first step to commit to your new career journey. The longest journey, as you've heard before, begins with one step.

What is your first commitment step?

Chapter 15 Exercises

Career Commitments, Part 1

1. What career-related commitments have you made to yourself in the past, but broken? Examples are meeting deadlines, staying at a job for a particular length of time, taking a course, passing an exam, or beginning your career change. *If the commitment is also to someone else, you should re-negotiate your commitment to them before doing the next steps.*

    a. Make a list of your commitments so that you can de-commit from them.

    b. After you have listed them, formally tell yourself that you are hereby released.

    c. Burn the paper and breathe.

2. Have you ever overstayed a commitment—that is, not de-committed even when the commitment was detrimental to you? What did you learn from the experience?

3. What can you use now from your prior commitment experiences? Would it be smart for you to move more slowly? Or do you need a push in taking bigger steps toward your goal?

4. Write in a journal or tell a friend what you now wish to commit to for your new career. Your commitment could be as simple as rereading this book or diving in to a particular chapter. Or maybe you will commit to tuning in, which is the most important stress-free technique of all. What is your commitment? Make sure it's chunked into a size you can accomplish.

Career Commitments, Part 2

1. By when will you start your commitment from the above exercise? When do you think you will complete it?

2. After completing the first step, decide if you wish to commit to another. If yes, what will that be?

Chapter 15 Summary

Wonderful! You have seen the importance of making a commitment to yourself. The simple way to realize your commitments is to look at your life. What do you do? This is what you are committed to. Is career change in the mix? If not, what is your commitment step—your first step on the journey?

A career commitment isn't an iron chain. De-committing is not only possible, but a part of life. There is always a way out.

***

If you are moving through the phases of making a career change, you might feel like a puppy yipping for her morning walk. But what if the time is not yet ripe for change? How can you live fully in the present when the future seems so much brighter? Join me in the next chapter as I learned how.

16:
Survive and Thrive

One day, on the last assignment of my project management career, I rushed to a nearby deli for lunch where I could have some privacy. I called a friend, and thankfully did not reach her voicemail.

"Help!" I said with no preamble. "I'm about to quit my job." Quickly I gave her the details.

My friend already knew that I had discovered, months ago, *the* topic. I had attended a speaker's conference where, at the first networking opportunity, someone asked me what I spoke about. Without even thinking (which is the way instinct works), I answered, "Women and career—how to enjoy or change a career without stressing out." After those words popped out I realized I had found it—my passion.

It made sense. Changing my career the first time had been an eight-year saga of confusion and fear, uncertainty and stress. Ultimately, I had found my way. And in the process, I had learned and practiced the three inner keys that would prevent the same mistakes from happening again. Eureka! This is what I wanted to write and talk about—career change the stress-free way.

Since that revelation, I threw myself into making what I said come true. As time passed, I felt so close to starting my own business that I could almost feel my toes wiggle as I worked barefoot at home. Work felt intolerable; I wanted to quit. I also needed someone to point out that I wasn't yet ready to say, "I quit!" out loud to my boss.

My friend did. During our lunchtime conversation she asked, "Marina, do you want the job you're at right now? Yes or no?"

I thought about it. I had not yet reached my financial goal that would let me take time off for the career change, nor had I completed gaining skills and trying on. I would need at least another year, maybe eighteen months.

"Yes, I want the job," I answered.

"Then go back and keep working," she said.

I did. I also realized that eighteen months was a long time to live in the future and not in the present. From that moment on, I practiced techniques that enabled me to both survive and thrive in the present.

Beginnings and Endings

In focusing on gracefully ending my soon-to-be-ex career, I was following an energetic principle. It is simple: beginnings and endings are very important. The energy of how we end one career affects the energy of how we begin the next. I wanted my next career's beginning to be spectacular, so I focused on making my present career's ending equally spectacular. All it took were three easy actions.

First, I recommitted to my present job. As much as I wanted to start my own company, the time was not yet ripe; my friend helped me to accept that fact. I intended to live in the present, not the future.

Second, I noticed the times—at first the many times—when I was not in the present. I caught myself planning and scheming in meetings, in meetings, and in meetings. Each time I noticed, I pulled myself back and re-engaged with, yes, the meeting.

Finally, I played games with myself to do the best possible job that I could. How could I work more efficiently? How could I produce the best possible document? How could I most efficiently do what my boss wanted? How could I communicate to my team members most effectively? How could I use my intuition more to help me more? From experience, I knew that doing an excellent job contributed to excellent energy.

After I got the hang of it myself, I explained the principle to Allison.

"If you were moving to a new apartment, would you pack all the dust balls and spider webs at your old apartment and bring them with you?" I asked Allison.

"Of course not!" she said. "And what's more, when I move, I usually throw out a lot of things that I don't want anymore. It's a good time to recycle and get rid of clutter."

"So, let's do the same thing now," I said. "Use noticing to see how you can get rid of unproductive habits and start new ones. See what you can do to equate your name with excellence—no matter how you are feeling or what you are doing."

And so she did.

Gratitude and Beauty

From my own experience, I knew that there were two other actions Allison could do to energize her ending. "What are you grateful for at this job?" I asked her. "What about it do you appreciate?"

She hesitated, and then answered, "The pay has certainly whittled down my student loans. And the location is fun. It's close to everything. And even though my boss is how she is, I have learned so much about myself from having to get along with her."

It was a start. I continued, "Do you think you could list five work-related things you are grateful about every day after work? On the subway coming home? Even when you are having a lousy day?"

"Even when I'm having a lousy day?" she replied.

I nodded. "One of my mentors put it this way: gratitude is the mother of faith. I think he's right. Practicing gratitude every day for what you have now—no matter what is happening—will give you the faith you need to continue your new career journey."

"What if I can't think of anything?" Allison asked.

"Then look around you to see what's beautiful. We are surrounded by beauty, inside and out. Even litter in the street can be artistic. If you look for beauty, you will find it everywhere, even on the subway. It's beautiful to see a teenage boy give up his seat to a pregnant woman. It's beautiful to feel your heart opening in joy."

To remind herself, Allison put these notes on her mirror at home:

> Beginnings and Endings are Important.

> What am I grateful for today?

What beauty did I see today? What beauty
did I create today?

Chapter 16 Exercises

Gratitude and Beauty

1. What are you grateful for about your current job? If you are not working, answer the same question for your last job or career.

2. Begin an everyday gratitude list. Writing the list on your way home from work is an excellent time. It will transform your day as you begin looking (and creating) incidents for which to be grateful.

3. At the same time, begin a beauty list. What did you see that was beautiful? What beauty did you create?

Past Endings

1. If you left a past job or career on a sour note, revisit the ending. Certainly, you did the best you could do at the time. But now, what would you do differently? What did you learn from the experience?

2. Do you need to forgive someone at that workplace? Forgive yourself? If so, write in your journal or tell a friend your story.

Current Ending

1. What can you do at work to make sure you leave your current job or career on a positive note? When will

you start these actions? (Hint: don't start your last week of work.)

2. Write in a journal or tell a friend what you will do. Check in with yourself, or ask your friend to hold you accountable for your changes.

Checklist of the Moving On Phase

You know the drill; please skip to the Summary if checklists don't work for you.

❏ I have tried on the careers from my Maybe List in the following ways:

_____

_____

❏ I am open to receiving intuitive information that might shortcut my career move.

❏ I know the mode by which I most frequently get intuitions.

❏ I check intuition against common sense.

❏ I am starting small in trusting my intuition.

❏ I have committed to at least one step in my career change.

❏ I understand that de-committing is possible.

❏ I am aware of what I am committing to in my life now.

❏ I understand the energetic principle of endings and beginnings.

❏ I have done the following to put this principle into motion:

_____

_____

❏ I am living in the present, not in the future.

Moving On Activities

See Figure 16-1 for Moving On Activities

Moving On Phase Activities
Figure 16-1

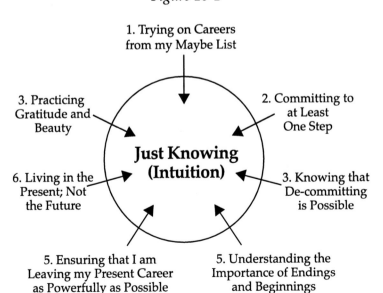

1. Trying on Careers from my Maybe List

2. Committing to at Least One Step

3. Practicing Gratitude and Beauty

Just Knowing (Intuition)

3. Knowing that De-committing is Possible

6. Living in the Present; Not the Future

5. Ensuring that I am Leaving my Present Career as Powerfully as Possible

5. Understanding the Importance of Endings and Beginnings

Chapter 16 Summary

Awesome, awesome, awesome! You have completed all three phases of the stress-free way to change your career—Discovery, Zooming In, and Moving On. In this chapter, we discussed the energy principle of beginnings and endings. The techniques Allison and I used to energize our career endings were: staying in the present, noticing when we were not, and perfecting excellence. Gratitude and seeing beauty will add to your ability to create a powerful beginning and ending. Figure 16-2 will remind you of all you've covered.

Stress-Free Career Change System
Figure 16-2

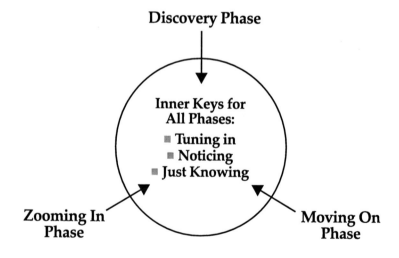

17:
Beyond
Moving On

Many thanks to my friends and those I've mentored for letting me relay their experiences. While their journeys continue, let's catch up with them.

***

When Allison assessed her values in the Discovery phase, she found that she wanted to be of help to children in some way. But instead of doing that immediately, Allison stayed at her marketing job for another year until she paid off her student loans. During the year, she continued to use Noticing to catch herself from caring too much what her boss thought about her. As she worried less about getting good-girl praise, she relaxed and even found herself, from time to time, enjoying her job—though not enough to stay in marketing.

Allison is now trying on a three-month volunteer job in a children's home. Following that experience, she will re-assess her direction and plan for her next steps.

***

Carmen partnered with someone to handle the business aspects of her jewelry business. The partnership allowed

Carmen to concentrate on her new creative venture, storytelling. She says that using her intuition helped her shortcut the time it took to break into her new career, as well as to build up the jewelry business. While Carmen cannot live on the revenues of just one of the businesses, the two together do support her. When she recalls that she once worked for a corporation, the memory feels to Carmen like something from a far distant past.

***

Rachel, the government manager, continues to tune in every day. She attributes that inner key to revitalizing her life. As she found out during Discovery, she did not want to leave her job. Instead, Rachel developed a business on the side that she could continue after she retired. Following one hunch after another, Rachel discovered a knack for building websites. As her inner geek and inner artist meet, Rachel feels confident that the web building business will challenge and fulfill her for years.

***

Tania is in her second year of teaching high school and loves it. Despite the paperwork, teaching gives her a sense of accomplishment and her students keep her laughing. She figures she must be doing something right, since so many of them happily shout out their greetings to her when she walks down the hallway.

But teaching isn't her only focus. Tania is also writing a screenplay at night and on the weekends. I'm counting on her to be the one to win that Oscar.

***

And me? After years of living in New York, I moved back to Northern California where my work career began. I started The Pink Edge, a company that empowers women in career change and enjoyment. Instead of changing careers completely, I juggle the new business while still managing software projects, finding that both bring me satisfaction in different ways and for different reasons. And as I did as a babysitter, I can again say that work is fun!

> Babysitting Lesson #2: Work can be fun!

Twists and Turns

When I was sorting tomatoes in the Sacramento Valley heat, did I ever think I would bundle up against the cold winds that freeze Wall Street? While working in the inner city of Oakland, did I conceive of consulting for the world's largest corporations? And while supporting myself in temp jobs, with waitress work on the side, did I imagine a day when I would live in a Manhattan penthouse and take taxis to work?

Well, the third one I did imagine. Among other goals, dreaming of a better financial day inspired me to succeed.

But there have been so many surprises. As you know, the path to finding my passion was not a straight line; it twisted and turned like a maze.

My intent is to "un-maze" the journey for you. But even following these steps, you are bound to run into a few surprises. At least, I hope you do.

You will also remember what it is like to be a beginner—again. Zen teacher Shunryu Suzuki said, "In the beginner's mind there are many possibilities, but in the expert's there are few."

While certainly true, his statement is the upside to being a beginner. I also found it humbling and scary to be a thirty-five-year-old beginner, and later a fifty-four-year-old one. But I wouldn't trade those beginnings and what I learned about myself for all the tea in Japan. I hope that you feel the same about the beginnings you will soon encounter.

***

One final piece of advice I would like to leave you with. As you move toward your new or expanded career and beyond, I encourage you to rely on the three inner keys of change:

- ✦ Draw power from your inner self.
- ✦ Notice what you are thinking, feeling, and doing.
- ✦ Let your intuition whisper; then listen and act.

Know that Life is helping you, as any Mother would, to learn and grow—even when you cannot possibly conceive of that being so.

All the best,

Marina

P.S. Don't forget one final babysitting lesson:

> Babysitting Lesson #7: Changing careers can be easy.

SPECIAL BONUS OFFER

As a thank you for purchasing *Make Every Day a Friday!* you are eligible for a free special report from The Pink Edge, *Ten Secrets of Stress-Free Living*.

These are not the every-day stress-management tips that you've heard again and again. Nor do they duplicate the stress-management suggestions on The Pink Edge website, www.pinkedge.com. These are inner secrets that come from Marina's twenty-five years of practicing meditation and mindfulness.

But don't worry; it won't take you twenty-five years to learn these methods. Marina has made the secrets easy to understand and to implement. And you don't have to know anything about meditation and mindfulness, or even be interested in those topics, to benefit.

How can you receive your free copy of *Ten Secrets of Stress-Free Living*? Just visit:

www.MakeEveryDayAFriday.com

You'll need to enter your name and email address to receive the report. Naturally, your privacy will be protected by The Pink Edge.

In advance, thank you for valuing your own health and well-being enough to take advantage of the special bonus offer, *Ten Secrets of Stress-Free Living.*

Appendix A: Marina's Paid Jobs

Like many people, I've had different jobs during my life. One day, I wrote them all down. See Table A-1 for the list I wrote. What an eye-opener! I feel grateful for the experiences, as I learned something from each job. And I'm also happy that some of them are in the past.

TABLE A-1:

Paid Jobs, Ages 11-30	
Babysitter	Peach sorter
Squash picker	Clerk
Tomato sorter	Fundraiser for non-profit
Waitress at a hamburger stand	Caseworker for county welfare department
Resident advisor in a dormitory	Coordinator for women's center
Peach picker	Community organizer and administrator

Paid Jobs, Ages 31–Now	
Telephone directory delivery person	Counter person at McDonald's
Paper delivery person	Program manager
Salesperson (selling inner tubes for truck tires)	Newspaper circulation district manager
Inventory counter at discount store	Cafeteria worker at summer Olympics
Technical writer	Computer programmer
Proofreader	Business analyst
Systems analyst	Housecleaner
Project manager	Word processor
Truck driver for newspaper	Database designer
Paralegal	Business owner
Temporary office worker	Waitress
Editor	Author, Trainer, Mentor & Speaker

Future: ???

Appendix B: Self-Discovery Resources

The additional resources for Self-Discovery (see chapter 5) are not career tests but quizzes about your personality, interests, values, and skills. Who are you right now?

Online Resources

(some are free in exchange for your email address; others charge a fee)

- ✦ www.9Types.com

- ✦ www.AdvisorTeam.com/user/kcs.asp (for the Keirsey Temperament Sorter)

- ✦ www.AnalyzeMyCareer.com

- ✦ www.CareerKey.org

- ✦ www.kolbe.com

- ✦ www.PassionPuzzle.com (not just for college students)

- ✦ www.Self-Directed-Search.com

Career Books with Self-Discovery Exercises

Changing Careers for Dummies: A Reference for the Rest of Us by Carol L. McClelland. See chapter 3 for self-discovery tests.

Do What You Are: Discover the Perfect Career for You Through the Secrets of Personality Type by Paul D. Tieger & Barbara Barron-Tieger.

What Color is Your Parachute? by Richard Bolles.

Other Books Helpful During a Career Change

Creative Visualization: Use the Power of Your Imagination to Create What you Want in Your Life by Shakti Gawain

Happy for No Reason: 7 Steps to Being Happy from the Inside Out by Marci Shimoff

The Passion Test by Janet and Chris Attwood

Unstoppable Women: Achieve ANY Breakthrough Goal in 30 Days by Cynthia Kersey

Appendix C: Money and Time Resources

These books are resources for bringing more money and time into your life (see chapter 9).

Money

Overcoming Underearning: Overcome Your Fears and Earn What You Deserve by Barbara Stanny

Prince Charming Isn't Coming: How Women Get Smart about Money by Barbara Stanny

Secrets of the Millionaire Mind: Mastering the Inner Game of Wealth by T. Harv Eker

Secrets of Six-Figure Women: Surprising Strategies to Up Your Earnings and Change Your Life by Barbara Stanny

Smart Women Finish Rich: 9 Steps to Achieving Financial Security and Funding Your Dreams by David Bach (see his other titles too)

Think and Grow Rich by Napoleon Hill

Women & Money: Owning the Power to Control Your Destiny by Suze Orman

Time

Never Check E-mail in the Morning: And Other Unexpected Strategies for Making Your Work Life Work by Julia Morgenstern

The 80/20 Principle: The Secret to Success by Achieving More with Less by Richard Koch

Time Management from the Inside Out by Julia Morgenstern

Acknowledgments

My appreciation extends to the friends, family, and mentors who helped me with this book. To my wonderful reviewers: Bette, Denise, Joan, Lisa, Lynn, and Tara, thank you. To Meredith Sue Willis and Hillary Hart: your comments were insightful and much appreciated. To other Pink Edge supporters who helped me during the writing: Alicia, Deborah, Earl, Gary, Irene, Les, Linda, Mary G., Sandy, Suzanne, and everyone in the Blue Pearl Group—thanks. Thanks also to my sisters, Charlotte and Sheryl, for your support.

Special thanks please to Ruth Caplin of Happy and Free Productions for your wisdom, clarity, artistic talent, and programming genius.

Another special thank you is for those I have mentored, especially in the Manhattan classes. Seeing us all change and grow has been fun, hasn't it?

Finally, to my teachers, mentors and friends, Sri Kaleshwar, Yuan Miao, and Rama: thank you for showing me, again and again, the stress-free way.

About the Author

Marina Spence founded The Pink Edge in 2007 to help women discover the joys and rewards of finding the right career.

Road tested during Marina's own years in the aggressive, fast-paced atmosphere of Wall Street, *Make Every Day a Friday!* has helped women navigate the intimidating and unsettling process of connecting who they are with what they do.

Marina grew up in the Central Valley of California, where she plunged into her first job—babysitting, followed by work in the fields. Since then, she has been a social worker, computer programmer, software project manager, and consultant for corporations like Morgan Stanley and JP Morgan Chase. She won professional accolades for her work with the New York City chapter of the Project Management Institute.

Marina's unique, holistic approach can help you discover the power of your inner Self. She has over twenty-five years experience with the #1 stress-buster, meditation, a foundation for discovering the deepest potentials of who we are and where we fit into the world.

Marina now lives and works in the San Francisco Bay Area.

Printed in the United States
148668LV00011B/3/P

9 781600 374500